Christine de Pizan's Letter of Othea to Hector

DATE DUE

The Focus Library of Medieval Women
Series Editor • Jane Chance

Christine de Pizan's Letter of Othea to Hector • Jane Chance • 1990

Forthcoming

Marguerite d'Oingt Writings • Renate Blumenfeld-Kosinski 1990
St. Bridget of Sweden Writings • Julia Bolton Holloway 1990
Cloistered Women: 14th Century German Convent Literature • Rosemary Hale • 1991
Hrotsvit of Gandersheim Legends • Katherina Wilson 1992

The Focus Classical Library
Series Editors • James J. Clauss and Michael Halleran

Hesiod's Theogony • Richard Caldwell • 1987
The Heracles of Euripides • Michael Halleran • 1988
Aristophanes' Lysistrata • Jeffrey Henderson • 1988

Forthcoming

Medea • A. J. Podlecki • 1989
Oedipus at Colonus • Mary Whitlock Blundell • 1990
Lucretius On The Nature of Things • Walter Englert • 1990
The Argonautica • James Clauss • 1991

Christine de Pizan's Letter of Othea to Hector

Translated
with Introduction, Notes,
and Interpretative Essay

Jane Chance
Rice University

First published 1990
Focus Information Group, Inc
Reissued 1997
D. S. Brewer, Cambridge

Transferred to digital printing

ISBN 978-0-85991-440-6

D. S. Brewer is an imprint of Boydell & Brewer Ltd
PO Box 9, Woodbridge, Suffolk IP12 3DF, UK
and of Boydell & Brewer Inc.
668 Mount Hope Ave, Rochester, NY 14604, USA
website: www.boydellandbrewer.com

A CIP catalogue record for this book is available
from the British Library

This publication is printed on acid-free paper

Table of Contents

In memory of my mother, Julia Mile Chance

Preface

L'*Epistre d'Othéa la deesse, que elle envoya a Hector de Troye quant il estoit en l'age de quinze ans* (*The Letter of the Goddess Othea, which She Sent to Hector of Troy when He Was Fifteen Years Old*) exists in forty-three extant manuscripts, powerful testimony to the public and courtly interest in this handbook of mythography written in 1399-1400 by the first French woman writer to earn her living by her pen; manuscripts of all of her works total at least two hundred. Unfortunately, because there is no critical edition on which to base a modern English translation from the French, I have decided to use the edition of Harley Ms. 4431 provided by Halina D. Loukopoulos in her 1977 dissertation (Wayne State University).[1]

There were cogent reasons behind Loukopoulos' decision to edit the most beautiful of all known manuscripts of the *Letter*. Gianni Mombello describes both it, and a second manuscript, B.N. fr. 606 (1405-6), as the most satisfying to its author;[2] Harley 4431 was also the last version known to have been approved by Christine (and was dedicated to Isabeau of Baveria).[3] Finally, Sandra Hindman's magisterial interdisciplinary study of politics and iconology identifies this same manuscript (and B.N. fr. 606) as the most useful for analysis of text in terms of manuscript illumination.[4]

This manuscript was probably completed no later than 1415. In Harley, the *Letter* appears in fols. 95r-141v, but the manuscript also

---

1 See Halina Didycky Loukopoulos, "Classical Mythology in the Works of Christine de Pisan, with an Edition of *L'Epistre Othea* from the Manuscript 4431" (Diss. Wayne State Univ. 1977).

2 Gianni Mombello, *La tradizione manoscritta dell' "Epistre Othea" di Christine de Pizan: Prolegomeni all'edizione del testo*, Memorie dell'Accademia delle scienze di Torino. Classe di scienze morali, storiche e filologiche, ser. 4a, n.15 (Turin: Accademia delle scienze, 1967), p. 302.

3 See Mombello, "Per un'edizione critica dell'"Epistre Othea' di Christine de Pizan," *Studi francesi*, 25 (1965), 2; and P.G.C. Campbell, *L'Épître d'Othéa: Étude sur les sources de Christine de Pisan* (Paris: Champion, 1924), pp. 19-23; Charity Cannon Willard thinks Christine herself made the corrections, in "An Autograph Manuscript of Christine de Pisan?" *Studi francesi*, 25 (1965), 454-55.

4 Millard Meiss, "The Exhibition of French Manuscripts of the XIII-XVI Centuries at the Bibliothèque Nationale," *The Art Bulletin*, 37 (1956), 193.

includes many of Christine's other works, among them, *L'Epistre au Dieu d'Amour (Cupid's Letter), Le Livre des trois jugements (Book of the Three Judgments), Le Chemin de long estude (The Long Road of Learning), Epistres sur le Roman de la Rose (Letters on the Romance of the Rose)*, and *Le Livre de la cité des dames (Book of the City of Ladies)*. On each folio two columns encompass between thirty-four and thirty-nine lines; the material is divided into Text, Gloss, and Allegory. One hundred thirty miniatures decorate the entire manuscript, with one hundred and one devoted to *Letter* alone (one for the *Prologue*, one each for the hundred chapters). Finally, the Harley miniatures, very like those in the Paris manuscript, were probably the work of an anonymous painter distinguished as "the Master of Christine de Pizan."[5]

Of Christine's works the *Letter* has been the most translated into English, beginning with Sir Stephen Scrope's Middle English translation, around 1450 (and dedicated to his stepfather Sir John Fastolf who had carried Ms. Longleat 253 back to England after serving in the 100 Years War), which is the translation published by the Early English Text Society in volume 260 and edited by Curt Bühler.[6] The early translators continued into the next century, with Anthony Babyngton basing his on Harley 838, in the later fifteenth century, and Robert Wyer, who around 1530 translated a version from the edition by Pigouchet known as *Les Cent histoires de Troye (The Hundred Histories of Troy)*.[7]

Editions of each of these translations appeared in print earlier in this century: in 1904, George F. Warner published the Stephen Scrope translation from the Marquis of Bath Longleat manuscript (London: J.B. Nichols), and in 1942, James D. Gordon edited a "Lytel Bibell of Knyghthod" (Babyngton's translation) based on Harley 838 for his University of Pennsylvania 1940 dissertation. Finally, Curt Bühler edited Scrope's translation based on St. Johns College, Cambridge, Ms. H.5., for an Early English Text Society edition in 1970 (vol. 264).

Given this long list of distinguished translators and editors, I am pleased to reintroduce this little known text into print and especially pleased that the text is intended for the classroom, wherein its thesaurus of mythology, catechism, allegory, and feminism will enrich students in all manner of courses. I like to imagine that Christine de Pizan, ever alert

---

5 Hindman, *Christine de Pizan's "Epistre Othea:" Painting and Politics at the Court of Charles VI* (Toronto: Pontifical Institute of Medieval Studies, 1986).

6 Although Bühler bases his edition on Ms. H.5 of St. John's College, Cambridge, there exists one other manuscript of the Scope translation. Bühler notes, p. xxvi, that the immediate French Ms. used by Scrope was probably a "sister-manuscript" of Ms. Laud Misc. 570 of the Bodleian, once owned by Falstof himself, according to Kathleen Chesney, "Two Manuscripts of Christine de Pisan," *Medium Aevum*, 1 (1932), 35-416.

7 (Paris: Philippe Pigouchet [1499-1500]).

to the need for education of princes and noble men and women, would also be pleased.

As an aid to the student, the Introduction includes in the first section a brief life of Christine and overview of her literary corpus, a second section which explains how Christine came to write a feminist mythography in reaction to the scholastic debate over the *Romance of the Rose*, a third section which traces the evolution of the interpretation of classical mythology in the Middle Ages and why it became so important to late medieval poets like Christine and Geoffrey Chaucer, and a fourth section which reveals Christine's innovations in mythography in the structure and frame of the *Letter*. To illustrate the reasons for the modern interest in Christine, the Interpretation at the end applies feminist theory to the myth of Minerva (Pallas Athena). Finally, the appendices diagram a medieval genealogy of the gods and list the major medieval mythographies and the Select Bibliography points the student to additional studies of mythography and poetic theory, feminist theory and studies of medieval women, and of Christine de Pizan.

To recover a meaning the closest to Christine's original—and thereby to reveal the frequent puns and images of which she is fond—my translation remains as nearly literal as possible. Notes at the bottom of the page will indicate the nature of such puns and images where translation blurs their interconnection within the text; all glosses, definitions, explanations, etc., in the text itself are Christine's. Her references to the Vulgate Bible are rendered by means of the Douay-Rheims translation. The titles for each individual fable have been added.

* * *

I am grateful to the Rockefeller Foundation and the magnificent Villa Serbelloni at Bellagio, on Lake Como in Northern Italy, where final polishing of the Introduction and Interpretation was completed during a month–long residency in July of 1988. I would also like to thank Judith Kellogg for her several readings of the Introduction and Interpretative Essay that resulted in helpful comments and criticisms, and Geraldine Heng, Renate Blumenfeld–Kosinski, and Laura McRae for their insights and comments on my argument. To C. Christine Salmon I am indebted for her work on the Prologue and the first fable. Julia Bernheim, at the Institute for Advanced Study, without complaint typed and retyped my text and prepared a preliminary index; I am also grateful to the English Department at Rice for retyping the text onto diskette. The dean of Humanities, Rice University, Allen Matusow, has supplied funds for the completion of the index. Finally, portions of the Interpretation appeared in the lecture I delivered at the Eleventh Annual Conference on Medieval Studies at Barnard College/Columbia University in New York, on "Minerva as Mother in Christine de Pizan's *Epistre d' Othéa*," on November 11th, 1989.

A Chronology of Christine de Pizan's Life, Times, and Works

1245? Guillaume de Lorris writes the *Romance of the Rose*.

1285-6? Jean de Meun writes his continuation of the *Romance of the Rose*.

1345? Geoffrey Chaucer is born in England.

1364 Christine is born in Venice.

1368-72 Chaucer writes his first major poem, *The Book of the Duchess*, as a visionary elegy for Blanche, the wife of John of Gaunt; he translates a portion of the *Romance of the Rose* into Middle English.

1369 The Benvenuto da Pizzano Family moves to Paris, where Tommaso, Christine's father, becomes court astrologer and physician to Charles V.

1378-80 Chaucer writes *The House of Fame*, an allegorical dreamvision about the vicissitudes of fame for the poet.

1379 Christine, 15, marries Etienne du Castel, secretary to Charles V.

1380 Charles V dies.

1380-2 Chaucer writes *The Parliament of Fowls*, a dream vision complaint and love-debate by the different species of birds.

1381 Christine, 17, gives birth to a daughter.

1382-1384 Christine's first son is born but dies.

1382-87 Chaucer translates Boethius's *Consolation of Philosophy* into Middle English, writes *Troilus and Criseyde*, and works on the *Legend to Good Women*.

1385 Christine, 21, gives birth to a second son.

1386 Tommaso de Pizan dies.

1388-92 Chaucer writes the *General Prologue* and the earlier tales in his major work of pilgrimage and social satire, *The Canterbury Tales*.

1389 Etienne du Castel dies.

1392-5 Chaucer completes most of the *Canterbury Tales*.

1386-1400 Chaucer finishes the latest tales, including the *Nun's Priest's Tale* and the *Parson's Tale*.

1399 Christine composes *L'Epistre au Dieu d'Amour* (*Cupid's Letter*), her first defense of women.

1399-1400 Christine writes *L'Epistre d'Othéa* (*The Letter of Othea to Hector*), a prose and verse epistolary mythography.

1400? Chaucer dies.

1400 Christine writes *Le Débat de deux amants* (*The Debate of the Two Lovers*), and "Dit de Poissy" ("Tale of Poissy"), two courtly–love debates.

1400-03 Christine writes *Le Livre de la mutacion de Fortune* (*The Mutation of Fortune*), an allegorical poem on fortune and universal history .

1402 Christine writes *Le Livre des trois jugements* (*The Book of Three Judgments*), verse, and *Le Dit de la Rose* (*The Tale of the Rose*), a debate about the *Order of the Rose*. She also writes *Le Chemin de long estude* (*The Long Road of Learning*), on universal empire .

1403 Christine writes *L'Epistre à Eustache Morel* (*Letter to Eustache Morel*), a letter to Deschamps on France's corrupt government.

1404 Christine writes *Le Livre des fais et bonnes meurs du sage roy Charles* (*The Deeds and Good Customs of the Wise King Charles*), a biographical history of Charles V.

1404-5 Christine writes *Le Livre de la cité des dames* (*The Book of the City of Ladies*), an allegorical poem.

1405 Christine writes *Le Livre des trois vertus* (*The Book of the Three Virtues*), an allegorical treatise on the virtues and sequel to *The Book of the City of Ladies*. She also completes *L'Avision-Christine* (*Christine's Vision*), her allegorical autobiography.

1405-6 Christine writes *Le Livre de la prod' hommie de l' homme* (*Book of Human Intregity*), on prudence and the cardinal virtues.

1406-7 Christine writes *Le Livre du corps de policie* (*Book of the Body Politic*), a Mirror of Princes handbook.

1410 Christine writes *Le Livre des fais d' armes et de chevalerie* (*Feats of Arms and of Chivalry*), a treatise on medieval warfare.

1412 Christine writes *Le Livre de la paix* (*The Book of Peace*), a treatise on the virtues.

1418 Christine retreats to the convent at Poissy.

1429 Christine completes her final work, *Le Ditié de Jehanne d'Arc* (*The Tale of Joan of Arc*), on the victory of Joan of Arc .

1430? Christine dies.

Introduction

I. The Life and Works of Christine de Pizan

In the Middle Ages (500-1500 A.D.), a handful of women, often associated with the court, began to write poems and works in the vernacular on topics outside the visionary autobiographical experience of the religious. This phenomenon started in the twelfth century—a time when native languages like French and English were developing written forms, in place of the dominant language of literacy, Latin. The Anglo-Norman Marie de France in the twelfth century composed *Lays*, *Fables*, and *St. Patrick's Purgatory* for a courtly audience; the Provençal Trobairitz Castelloza, from Auvergne, also of the twelfth century, wrote courtly lyrics, and the Spanish Florencia Pinar in the late fifteenth century adopted the *canso*, or secular song, as her own, again, with a characteristic courtly bent. And there was, of course, the very influential Franco-Italian woman poet and scholar Christine de Pizan (1364-1430?).

The first French woman poet to make her living by the pen, the first female mythographer (interpreter of classical myths), and first female literary theorist, Christine held enormous power in the French court and influenced late medieval culture—in France and in England—in a number of ways. Christine's influence in England was considerable: copies were made of her manuscripts, her poem *L'Epistre au Dieu d'Amour* (*Cupid's Letter*) influenced Hoccleve's *Letter of Cupid* and William Worchester paraphrased *Le Livre des fais d'armes et de chevalerie* (*Feats of Arms and of Chivalry*) in his *Boke of Noblesse*. Various English nobles had her works copied and translated, among them Henry IV, Henry VII, Edward IV, Lord Salisbury, and the Earl Rivers; they were translated not only into English but even into Portuguese—the *Le Livre des trois vertus* (*The Book of the Three Virtues*) was translated by request of Queen Isabel of Portugal.[1] Of her twenty-three works, few of which are available in translation today, Christine's most popular was the *Letter of Othea to Hector*, a mythographic manual full of allegories of the gods normally accessible only to the formally educated. How did this astonishing and prolific

---

1 See P. G. C. Campbell, "Christine de Pisan en Engleterre," *Revue de littérature comparée*, 5 (1925), 659-70.

woman achieve so much, given her lack of formal education and of any tradition of women writing secular materials, and living in times parlous by any definition?

France, like England in the fourteenth and early fifteenth centuries, existed in an era of turmoil, instability, war, sickness, and death—a time in many ways like the twentieth century. The Hundred Years War between France and England had decimated the aristocracy and ravaged the countryside. The repeated cycles of the Black Death (the plague) during the fourteenth century, when millions died, attacked families regardless of their social class. The mini-Ice Age, early in the century when temperatures dropped dangerously below normal levels and prevented planting of crops, resulted in famines, which led to economic privation and further unease, most noticeably in the uprising of the lower classes known as the Peasants' Revolt (1381). The authority of the Church—there was only one faith in the Middle Ages, the Catholic faith—had been badly undermined by the "Babylonian Captivity" in the early fourteenth century, when the French established their own Papal seat at Avignon, instead of the Italian Papal seat at the Vatican, which resulted in two Popes. Spiritual values seemed to be in decline, accompanied by the disintegration of political and social values founded on those spiritual values which had been accepted as stable and enduring from the earliest of times.

Rather ironically, in Italy, and then in France and England, this turbulence was accompanied by a brilliant outpouring of verse and prose in the vernacular. In Italy, beginning with Dante Alighieri, Francis Petrarch, and Giovanni Boccaccio in the fourteenth century, this Renaissance was followed in France with poets (and musicians) like Guillaume de Machaut, Jean Froissart, and Eustace Deschamps, and in England with the *Pearl*-Poet, Geoffrey Chaucer, and William Langland. Reflecting this discontent and disintegration of cultural and religious values, their works are full of satire, irony, and paradox, or incongruity. The poet often used his courtly position to reflect (and warn against) the enormous changes in society and culture. Within this larger literary and cultural context it seems especially odd to find a woman poet reacting to these changes—for typically women of that time could neither read nor write.

Because usually only consecrated religious women, especially in the period up to the thirteenth century, received a literary education in the convents (but never in the cathedral and university schools of the later Middle Ages), it is most remarkable that Christine, self-taught as she was,

was encouraged to read—very much like the modern Virginia Woolf—by her father. It is true that, beginning in the thirteenth century, laywomen might be taught to read and write in the vernacular, perhaps to run a large household, or to help with a family business, but they did not learn Latin or Greek.[2] And throughout the Middle Ages, literacy—by which is meant Latin literacy—remained a necessity for the writer and scholar.

Of the known women writers in the Middle Ages and early Renaissance, most were visionaries and mystics drawn to the religious experience of the convent and the opportunity to know God. Such an orientation characterized the rare woman writer capable of writing in Latin. In the eighth century, Anglo-Saxon Hugeberc of Hildesheim (she died in Germany) chronicled the life of a male saint in her *Hodoeporicon of St. Willibald*; in the ninth century, the Frankish Dhuoda wrote a *Manual*; and in the tenth century, the Saxon Hrotsvit of Gandersheim composed plays and Christian epics in Latin. To these figures, add Heloise writing her letters to Abelard in the twelfth century and the German visionary Hildegard of Bingen, whose autobiography reflected her epiphanies; like Hildegard, German nuns of the thirteenth century wrote down their visions—St. Elisabeth of Schönau, Mechthild of Magdeburg and St. Gertrude the Great at the convent of Hefta, and Mechthild of Hackeborn.

Even with the rise of the vernacular in the twelfth and thirteenth centuries, women writers generally remained ecclesiasts who created their own form, the spiritual autobiography or life, and injected into this most personal of genres a sensibility that is characteristically female. We find, in addition to the visionaries writing in German, others writing in Dutch or Brabant—Hadewijch and Beatrijs of Nazareth—and, in Italian, the writers of spiritual lives, St. Clare and St. Agnes of Assisi. Another Italian, St. Umiltà of Florence, wrote her sermons in Latin and the Blessed Angela of Foligno dictated in Italian. Even in the fourteenth century, the role of the visionary and the spiritual or visionary autobiography remained the most familiar activity for a woman writer, largely because a woman either married and had children or she entered a convent—there was no other experience available. So in France we have Marguerite Porete, writing *The Mirror of Simple Souls Who Are Annihilated*; Marguerite d'Oingt, who wrote autobiographical works and works of spiritual guidance such as *The Page of Meditation* and *The Mirror* in Latin; the Provençal Na Prous Boneta and her autobiographical confession; the Swedish mystic St. Bridget; the Tuscan saint, Catherine of Siena, who dictated letters in

---

2   See, for example, Joan M. Ferrante, "The Education of Women in Theory, Fact, and Fantasy," in *Beyond their Sex: Learned Women of the European Past*, ed. Patricia Labalme (New York: New York University Press, 1980), pp. 9-42; and Eileen Power, *Medieval Women*, ed. M. M. Postan (Cambridge: Cambridge Univ. Press, 1975), pp. 76-88.

Italian and wrote a *Dialogue*; and of course the betterknown English visionary mystics, Julian of Norwich in her *Showings* and Margery Kempe in her *Book*, or the Spanish Doña Leonor López de Córdoba with her *Memories*. And in the fifteenth century we find Magdalena Beutler of Freiburg who wrote in German *The Book of the Experience of the Truly Faithful* and the Dutch work of spiritual guidance attributed to Anna Bijn, *Mary of Nijmeghen*.

To a large extent, Christine's family background and the temper of the times enhanced her self-education and her purpose in writing. Both of these factors came to be interrelated: her father held an important position at court and the king at that time, Charles V, placed a humanistic and liberal emphasis on books and education. The first child of Tommaso di Benvenuto da Pizzano, Christine was born in Venice in 1364; because his family had been connected with the small town of Pizzano near Bologna, his name was gallicized five years after he became court astrologer and physician, that is, the year he moved five-year-old Christine and her mother from Venice to Paris.[3] Tommaso had studied medicine and theology at the University of Bologna and may even have instructed as a professor (only later serving as councillor of Venice); for this reason he encouraged Christine to read the books in his library, and so she became educated in French, English, Italian, and Latin while he remained at court for ten years.

Nevertheless, her family circumstances would have most likely prevented her from achieving much more, except for a series of unfortunate events which changed her life. In 1379, at 15, Christine had married Etienne du Castel, secretary to Charles V, who continued in the post after Charles died in 1380 (although her father thereafter lost influence and became dependent on her husband). In 1381, at the age of seventeen, she gave birth to the first of her three children, a daughter, and then, in the next four years, to two sons, one of whom died; the youngest was born in 1385, when Christine was 21. As if this were not enough to still whatever creative and scholarly impulses she may have felt, in 1386 her father died, followed, three years later, when she was 25, by her husband. In itself this unhappy circumstance should not have catalyzed her writing career. But because lawyers afterwards cheated her out of her inheritance, and because she was left to support not only her children but also her mother, a brother, and a niece, she was compelled, first, to become a scribe and manuscript copyist, and then to take up the pen herself. As strange as this must have seemed at the time, she regarded her new career as a kind of helpful and even necessary mutation: in 1400-1403, in the visionary *Le Livre de la mutacion de Fortune (The Book of the Mutation of Fortune)*,

---

3   See Elena Nicolini, "Cristina da Pizzano (L'origine e il nome)," *Cultura Neolatina*, Anno I, fasc. 2 (1941), 143-50.

she imagines herself transformed into a man in both body and will by the allegorical personification Fortune, so that she can better function in the world.

Whatever her fantasy or the source of her strength, it resulted in a prodigious outpouring of works, both verse and prose, on moral, political, and educational philosophy; religion; etiquette; medieval warfare; autobiography and biography; literary theory; mythography; courtly love; and the history, defense, and education of women. Her fifteen volumes of work are contained in some seventy notebooks and span thirty years, from 1399-1429. For all practical purposes, her writing career ended when she retreated to the convent in 1418, probably Poissy, where her daughter served as a nun, for her penultimate work was written some six years before the retreat, in 1412.

Unusual as it is to find a woman poet in the late Middle Ages, it is more unusual to find one who was also a scholar. Excluded from conventional schooling, later in her life Christine was accused of faulty Latin and Greek in writing her major mythographic work (and therefore of revising the mythographic tradition out of ignorance rather than by intention). As a scholar she was marginalized even after her death, through her incredulous translators. Ironically, in the mid-fifteenth century, Stephen Scrope claims that her work _The Epistle of Othea to Hector, or, the Boke of Knyghthode_, was in fact composed by the doctors of the University of Paris because the "wise gentlewoman Dame Cristine of France"—Christine de Pizan—had prayed they do so. Pigouchet's translation does not mention her at all, nor does Wyer's. It was apparently so convincing in its scholarship and erudition that its translators, and later its publishers, doubted that it could have been written by a woman. Indeed, the _Letter of Othea to Hector_ is one of her first works, written about 1399-1400, and, in its specific treatment of the classical gods, is fairly conventional. Nevertheless, even this early and very popular work (indeed, most popular of all her works in Christine's day) reflects her originality and underlying feminism, which are clear to readers of Christine today. Evidently, the way its readers approach the text determines its specific meaning and its importance. To perceive both its historical significance and its contemporary relevance depends upon an understanding of the cultural context in which it was written and the extent to which emotional and scholarly debates over literary theory dictated stages in Christine's own career as a writer and scholar and the development of her philosophical views concerning women, education, and politics.

Her early works adopt the conventional forms and themes of courtly love (that is, the aristocratic game of romantic love, with its worship of the lady as a goddess by the much-suffering and excessively devoted lover). But the later works move toward more philosophical and educational topics. Her earliest poems—highly structured and artificial forms such as lays, rondeaus, *balades*, debates, and love-complaints—appeared over a six-year period, but were collected by another hand in the late fourteenth century for an anthology of her poems known as the *Cent ballades d'amant et de dame (One Hundred Ballades of a Lover and his Lady)*. Some of these lyrics reflect Christine's grief over her husband's early death, whereas others involve love, knights, chivalry, and the conventional postures of courtly love. Courtly love, the precursor of modern romantic love, was an artificial and aristocratic form of love playfully practiced in the courts by lovers who performed chivalric feats to earn the favor of ladies they adored as goddesses. Initiated in the twelfth century by troubadour poets at the court of Eleanor of Aquitaine and expressed in allegorical form in the thirteenth-century by Guillaume de Lorris in the influential *Romance of the Rose*, courtly love as the subject of verse also affected Christine's literary practice, as we shall see. Indeed, her first major work, *Cupid's Letter* (1399), was a feminist reply to Jean de Meun's thirteenth–century misogynistic continuation of the *Romance*, in which Cupid receives the complaints of women about deceitful men, carries these complaints to an assembly of gods, and lectures men against unchivalrous behavior.

The courtly themes continue in *Le Débat de deux amants* (*The Debate of the Two Lovers*, c. 1400) in which Christine argues with two men, a *chevalier* (knight) and *écuyer* (squire), who may have had unhappy love affairs. According to one, love attacks reason, according to the other, love ennobles. There are other debates penned by Christine, among them, "Dit de Poissy" ("The Tale of Poissy," 1400). Written after a trip to the Dominican abbey at Poissy where her daughter was a nun, the debate compares the suffering of a girl whose lover has been captured by the enemy to that of a squire rejected by a lady. *Le Livre des trois jugements* (*The Book of Three Judgments*, c. 1402) also concerns three cases involving love, brought to the Sénéchal of Hainault by three plaintiffs. *Le Dit de la Rose* (*The Tale of the Rose*, 1402) is a tribute to the Burgundian Court of Love and the charade presented on Valentine's Day in 1402 by the Duke of Orleans. In this tale, the goddess Loyauté (Loyalty) is sent by the god of love to initiate an Order of the Rose for chivalrous knights who promote women's honor. In a interesting convergence of art and reality, within the text the same personification of Loyalty then awakens the poet Christine after the festivity to ask her to found an order herself. Finally, *Le Livre du duc des vrais amants* (*The Book of the Duke of True Lovers*), 1405, a courtly romance, involves the "Duke of True Lovers" and his affair with a married princess, both of whom write poems during a separation.

As her career developed, Christine discarded courtly love themes and became more interested in education, perhaps because she herself, as a noblewoman, had been denied a formal education. She focuses on the education of the head of state, the individual knight, and women. *Le*

Chemin de long estude (*The Long Road of Learning*, 1402-3), a didactic allegory (6392 lines), is a dream vision in which Christine is guided by the Cumaean Sibyl, the same oracle who appears before Virgil's Aeneas to help him descend into the underworld (whose entrance was believed by the ancients to be located not far from Cumae in the province of Campania, in Italy). Unlike Aeneas, Christine tours the world along the "road of long study," finally ascending to heaven. The court of Raison (Reason) is reached after the mysteries of the firmament are explored. Four queens rule the world in this court—Noblesse (Nobility), Chevalerie (Chivalry), Richesse (Riches), and Sagesse (Wisdom), with Reason as queen of all. Through them Christine learns how to remedy the evils of the world: a court of earthly judges will select a universal monarch based on the goals of the four goddesses, and the universal monarch will establish peace and justice on earth. Thereafter, Christine, Reason's messenger, awaits the decision of the French princes (the earthly judges), awakening when her mother knocks on the door—as if the decision were imminent in the real world as well.

Also to aid the body politic, she wrote another work on education, in particular, of the dauphin (the eldest son of the king of France), although she also touches on government, French society, and peace, in *Le Livre de la paix* (*The Book of Peace*, 1412-13). Further, *Le Livre du corps de policie* (*The Book of the Body Politic*, 1406-7), a political work of moral overlay, was again intended to educate the dauphin, Louis de Guyenne, in the roles of the three estates in the body politic (she uses the plan derived from John of Salisbury's *Policraticus*). Here she reveals her belief in the hereditary monarchy, with her ideal as Charles V; she imagines the body politic as having a head (king), hands and arms (knights and nobles), and feet (commoners), who support the whole edifice. She also wrote to Isabeau of Bavaria pleading for peace on October, 1405, when France teetered on the brink of civil war, in "Une Epistre à Isabeau de Baviére" ("A Letter to Isabeau of Bavaria"), a letter probably intended for Isabeau's brother-in-law and companion, Louis d'Orleans.

Her educational philosophy for women is expressed in the didactic works of *Le Livre de la cité des dames* (*The Book of the City of Ladies*), *The Book of Three Virtues*, and *The Long Road of Learning*.[4] As a sequel to *The Book of the City of Ladies*, *The Book of Three Virtues* concerns the education of women of all classes, ages, and situations. Here Reason, Righteousness, and Justice are joined by Prudence to instruct women divided into three groups (queens and ladies, noblewomen, and com-

---

4 See Astrik L. Gabriel, "The Educational Ideas of Christine de Pisan," *Journal of the History of Ideas*, 16 (January, 1955), 3-21. She also knew about medieval medicine and healing: see Muriel Joy Hughes, *Women Healers in Medieval Life and Literature* (New York: King's Crown, 1943), pp. 37, 41-2.

moners) in moral and practical lessons which range from advice on handling servants when husbands are absent to counsel on how to love spouses.

It is clear from this brief overview that Christine's long and full career as a writer developed in large part from the benevolent support of an educated father and a humanistic king, coupled with adverse financial and personal circumstances. What is less clear is why her work changed so from its early reflection of the themes of courtly love, made especially popular by the thirteenth-century *Romance of the Rose* and many other French and English poems, to a broader, more philosophical vision of society and woman's role within that society. Many of Christine's works seem to derive less from any embrace of the courtly tradition than from her reaction to the antifeminism she found there, as well as from her determination to educate women, the dauphin, and her son in the best manner she knew.

It is possible that Christine's vision grew in part from her desire to rewrite the genealogy of the gods from a female perspective in the *Letter of Othea*, which seems to have coincided with her participation in the scholarly debate over the *Romance of the Rose*. She supposedly finished *The Letter of Othea to Hector* in 1399-1400, just before the "Quarrel of the Rose" in 1400-2; afterwards, in 1405, she wrote the allegorical *Book of the City of Ladies*. Most fascinating in tracing the origin of her feminism—and the reasons for her interest in mythography—is her reaction—among other issues concerning the work's immorality—to the final, pornographic seizure and penetration of the budding rose in Jean de Meun's continuation of Guillaume's *Romance*.

II. The Origins of Christine's Gynocentric Mythography: The Debate over the *Rose*

Although the *Romance of the Rose*, as an allegorical and courtly poem, was enormously popular in the Middle Ages (especially the unfinished early thirteenth-century portion by Guillaume de Lorris), it was as a didactic and satiric encyclopedia, in Jean de Meun's Aristotelian continuation in the later thirteenth century, that it most affected the course of literary theory. The question for the reader, whether contemporary with Christine or with us, remains the same: is this poem meant to be read literally or figuratively? Is Jean a misogynist, or, more important, was it acceptable for Jean to hold misogynist views?

In Guillaume's version, the thirteenth-century account of courtly love begins with a walled garden, what was termed a *hortus conclusus*, whose door is opened to the Lover by Idleness, or the porter Oiseuse. By means of this entry, the Lover meets the garden's inhabitants, who are named for what they signify about courtly love—Leisure, Beauty, Youth, etc. The garden itself, however, is dominated by a Well of Narcissus in which the

Lover peers to catch the distorted reflection of the lady (or himself). The poet seems to imply that courtly love, in its sloth and narcissism, represents a hothouse form of *amor sui*, or perverse self-love—selfishness. Continuing this idea more openly and cynically, Jean de Meun presents the Lover as selfishly armed by Love's barons in order to assault (seduce) the Rose. In the game of courtly love, to win the lady's favor (personified in the character Fair Welcome—Bel Acueil) he must overcome the character Evil Tongue (Malebouche) by assuming the guise of the character False-Seeming (Faus Semblant)—that is, by presenting his nefarious intentions as good.

It is the ending and how it was meant to be interpreted which partly triggered the fifteenth-century debate over the *Romance*. Jean de Meun conceives of the Lover's desire for the rose as a literal, sexual desire, its fulfilment evisaged as an erotic deflowering, petal by petal. In the final description of the seduction of the rose, Jean's Lover imagines his phallus pressing against the hymeneal barrier as a knight jousting against an evil adversary. In the Lover's description of his seduction, his "chivalric protagonist" is compared with the Greek hero Hercules in his battle against Cacus, whose name means "evil" and whom Hercules confronts in one of his twelve labors.

I kissed the image very devoutly and then, to enter the sheath safely, wished to put my staff into the aperture, with the sack hanging behind. Indeed I thought that I could shoot it in at the first try, but it came back out. I replaced it, but to no avail; it still recoiled. By no effort could it enter there, for, I found, there was a paling in front, which I felt but could not see. It had formed the fortification of the aperture, close to its border, from the time when it was first built; it gave greater strength and security.

I had to assail it vigorously, throw myself against it often, often fail. If you had seen me jousting—and you would have had to take good care of yourself—*you would have been reminded of Hercules when he wanted to dismember Cacus.* He battered at his door three times, three times he hurled himself, three times fell back. His struggle and labor were so great that he had to sit down three times in the valley, completely spent, to regain his breath. I had worked so hard that I was covered with the sweat of anguish when I did not immediately break the paling, and I was indeed, believe it, as worn out as Hercules, or even more. Nevertheless, I attacked so much that I discovered a narrow passage by which I thought I might pass beyond, but to do so I had to break the paling. By this path, narrow and small, where I sought passage, I broke down the paling with my staff and gained a place in the aperture. (Dahlberg, pp. 351-2; my italics.)

Christine de Pizan expressed her own view of the *Romance of the Rose* of Jean de Meun in a series of letters which form part of the *Querelle de la Rose (Debate over the Rose)* (1400-02). Apparently, after she had referred to the *Romance* in an uncomplimentary fashion in her early work, *Cupid's Letter* (1399), Jean de Montreuil, Provost of Lille, sent a copy of the commentary on the *Romance* that he wrote after reading it in the spring of 1401. In her response to the provost, full of the research she had just completed for the *Letter of Othea*, Christine finds the ravishing of the rose in the *Romance* anti-feminist and the poem's rehearsal of vice (which the poet supposedly abhors) immoral enticement. She surmises that "the great lechery which obsessed him [Jean] perhaps made him more prejudiced than profitable, as by our actions our inclinations commonly reveal themselves" (Willard, in Wilson, pp. 344-5), Jean's prejudice depends upon a view of women as vicious and immoral. In protest she notes (as she does in both the *Letter* and *City of Ladies*) that

...there have nevertheless been, are now, and will always be women more valiant, more honest, better bred, and even wiser, and through whom more good has come to the world, than has ever come from him [Jean de Meun].... There are many examples of these in the Bible and other ancient histories, such as Sarah, Rebecca, Esther, Judith, and others, and even in our own times we have seen in France many valiant ladies, great and noble French women: the saintly, devout Queen Jeanne, Queen Blanche, the duchess of Orléans who was the king of France's daughter, the duchess of Anjou, who is now known as the queen of Sicily, and others besides who were beautiful, chaste, honest, and wise, and also lesser noblewomen such as milady of La Ferté, wife of Pierre de Craon, who are also greatly to be praised.... (Willard, in Wilson, pp. 343-4.)

Christine's ire no doubt prompted the writing of her *Book of the City of Ladies* several years later.

Paramount among the important issues that concerned Christine in this debate are the immorality and the dishonesty of the work, especially when the falsity and immorality involve women. She objects in particular to the false counsel of the character Reason and the immorality of others, including the figure Genius (an allegorical personification of human nature, particularly in its generative urges) and his graphic images of human genitalia. Underlying her criticism of the work is an implicit understanding of the reading process as grounded in the literal meaning of the text. Both of these issues would concern her for the rest of her life.

De Meun's advocate, Jean de Montreuil, however, defended the poem—as *fabula*, a fictional book about jealous husbands with souls out of kilter. He was joined by other scholars, Pierre and Gantier Col, in the debate. Accustomed in their schools to reading narratives which say one thing but mean another, medieval scholars might very well stereotype Christine's reading as "female"—illiterate and literalistic, or envious, proud, vicious, in short, in its adherence to the letter rather than the spirit. Indeed, Jean de Meun's own female character Reason defends the use of figurative interpretation of parables:

> In our schools indeed they say many things in parables that are very beautiful to hear; however, one should not take whatever one hears according to the letter. In my speech there is another sense, at least when I was speaking of testicles, which I wanted to speak briefly here, than that which you want to give to the word. He who understands the letter would see in the writing the sense which clarifies the obscure fable. The truth hidden within would be clear if it were explained. You will understand it well if you review the integuments of the poets. There you will see a large part of the secrets of philosophy. There you will want to take your great delight, and you will thus be able to profit a great deal. You will profit in delight and delight in profit, for in the playful fables of the poets lie very profitable delights beneath which they cover their thoughts when they clothe the truth in fables. If you want to understand my saying well, you would have to stretch your mind in this direction.
>
> But afterward I pronounced these two words—and you understood them well—which should be taken quite strictly according to the letter, without gloss. (Dahlberg, ll. 7153-83, p. 136.)

Jean here reminds his audience of the scholastic technique of *fabula*, fable or parable, in composing poetry. He also refers to the "integuments of the poets," indicating his familiarity with mythographic exegesis as it was practiced in the schools to help clerics learn Latin grammar by means of poems like Ovid's *Metamorphoses*.

Note, however, that Reason justifies her literal use of the two words ("penis" and "testes") to which the Lover has objected as bawdy and obscene. In this case, the words express what is natural and therefore good because they are made by God to ensure the survival of the species. This philosophical issue about the intrinsic goodness of Nature, of course, will lead the reader into the moral dilemma posed by the Lover's seduction of the rose: is he motivated by the desire for sexual pleasure, or for procreation (allowable in the Middle Ages only within the sacramental context of marriage)? That the Lover objects to Reason's use of words for things as bawdy, but fails to see what he does as dehumanizing and immoral—bawdy indeed—brings us back to the debate about letter and figure.

The philosophical debate was essentially a scholastic one, growing out of the universities, and therefore one from which Christine, as a woman barred from either learning or teaching at a university, would have been excluded. The philosophical allegory of Jean's continuation, reflecting as it does the advent of the "new Aristotelianism" uncovered by Averroes and the other Arabic translators, affected aesthetic theory in the fourteenth and fifteenth centuries by rehearsing the Realist/Nominalist controversy in poetry: is a word the same as a thing or a symbol of a thing? And therefore is it real, or only the name of a real thing? If words are real, must we then read the text literally, or can we read figuratively, as Augustine counseled in *De doctrina Christiana (On Christian Doctrine)*—to lift our thoughts from the "body" of the text to its "spirit"? Is the assault on the rose at the end of the *Romance* a "beautiful parable" that hides truths, or is it in itself erotic?

Part of the problem in unraveling this complex issue concerns the double nature of the classical poet whom Jean mimicks in his continuation of the *Romance*. His continuation is often termed Ovidian, meaning heavily influenced by the classical poet Ovid (b. 43 B.C.), most likely in *Ars Amatoria (Art of Love)*. Because courtly love was, in part, a medieval interpretation and adaptation of the kind of predatory erotic love articulated in Ovid's "educational" treatise (on the "art" of love), it never completely lost its underlying erotic bias, no matter how disguised by the courtly and aristocratic mask it wore. As an example of how Jean incorporates Ovid, let us consider the classical poet's stock figure Duenna, an old woman whose cynical love advice for younger women depends upon stratagems and deceits. She is apparently mirrored in Jean de Meun's La Vieille (Old Woman), who encourages women to establish deceitful defenses against deceitful men. The Old Woman in Jean de Meun voices sympathy for women lovers and antipathy for the men who betray them; she remarks that Phyllis suffered for Demophoon, as Oenone suffered for Paris and Medea for Jason.

Briefly, all men betray and deceive women; all are sensualists, taking their pleasure anywhere. Therefore we should deceive them in return, not fix our hearts on one. Any woman who does so is a fool; she should have several friends and, if possible, act so as to delight them to the point where they are driven to distraction. If she has no graces, let her learn them. Let her be haughtier toward those who, because of her hauteur, will take more trouble to serve her in order to deserve her love, but let her scheme to take from those who make light of her love. She should know games and songs and flee from quarrels and disputes. If she is not beautiful, she should pretty

herself; the ugliest should wear the most coquettish adornments. (Dahlberg, ll. 13265-13282, p. 229.)

Unfortunately, the Old Woman herself is a cunning, misogynistic creation—a parody of all that is evil in women.

And yet Ovid wrote a poem seemingly more sympathetic to women
in his *Heroides*, in which he uses the fiction of betrayed women writing
letters to those men who have abandoned them—women like Laodamia,
Phyllis, Canacee, Cydippe, Hero. If we trace the question of the importance of the literal level of meaning as opposed to the figurative level of
meaning far enough into the past, we still return to the same question: to
decide whether a poet is sympathetic to women or is instead misogynistic,
we must ask, does he intend his narrative and characterization to be
literally true, or to be ironic, that is, meaning something other than what
he actually says? Meaning according to the letter of the text, called *littera*
in Latin, also denotes the sign or word, and in the plural refers to epistles.
And what then does Ovid mean by using the form of the epistle, the letter,
in apparent defense of women? And what then does Christine mean when
she writes her *Epistre d'Othéa*, her "Epistle" or "Letter" of Othea to
Hector?

In England, writing fifteen or twenty years before Christine, the
important court poet Geoffrey Chaucer (1345?-1400?), in his *Legend of
Good Women* (a poem which Christine much admired), signals his own
ambivalence over the question of how to read the *Romance*. In the dream
vision prologue to this collection of *Heroides*-like tales of women martyred for love, the God of Love accuses Chaucer of heresy against love.
The charges grow out of the poet's Middle English translation of the
courtly and lascivious French *Romance* of Guillaume de Lorris and also
out of his "falsing" of the Trojan woman Criseyde—representing, in
effect, all women who change their minds in loving—in Chaucer's
psychological romance, *Troilus and Criseyde*. Chaucer the poet projects
his ambivalence toward women in the *Legend* by portraying one part of
himself, the conscientious and feminist God of Love, as sternly admonish-
ing the apparently misogynistic character of "Chaucer." The God argues
that:

> You are my mortal foe and wage war against me,
> And you slander my old servants,
> And hinder them with your translation,
> And turn away folk who are devoted
> To serving me, and hold it folly
> To trust in me. You may not deny it,
> For in plain text, which needs no glossing,
> You have translated the *Romance of the Rose*—
> That is a heresy against my law.
> And you make wise folk withdraw from me,

And think in your sense, which is truly cold,
That he is a truly proper fool
Who loves paramours too hard and too hotly.
(Benson, G248-60, my trans.)

Even when the contrite protagonist Chaucer follows the God of Love's prescribed penance of writing legends of good women later in the *Legend*, he draws them in part from the suspect Ovidian work, the *Heroides*—including Dido, Medea, Hypsipyle, Ariadne. Even today scholars puzzle over Chaucer's intention in retelling these fables: does he literally invite our sympathy for these women, or is he slanting the retelling so as to cast aspersions on them? It is therefore not surprising that a woman reading Chaucer—or Jean, or Ovid—in the fourteenth or fifteenth centuries might have read them differently from contemporary educated male scholars and poets.

Although barred from a formal education which might have trained her in glossing Ovid, Christine did read the *Ovide moralisé* (*Ovid Moralized*), a fourteenth-century Ovid commentary, to which she was indebted for many of the fables in her *Letter of Othea*. But she was also familiar with the misogyny of both contemporary and ancient scholars and poets. In *The Book of the City of Ladies*, Christine postures as a woman reader confronting images of women as inferior, negligent, and vicious in a text written by a man—one Mathéolus, in his *Lamentations*.

> But just the sight of this book, even though it was of no authority, made me wonder how it happened that so many different men—and learned men among them—have been and are so inclined to express both in speaking and in their treatises and writings so many wicked insults about women and their behavior. Not only one or two and not even just this Mathéolus (for this book had a bad name anyway and was intended as a satire) but, more generally, judging from the treatises of all philosophers and poets and from all the orators—it would take too long to mention their names—it seems that they all speak from one and the same mouth. They all concur in one conclusion: that the behavior of women is inclined to and full of every vice.

Immediately thereafter Christine sinks into a deep depression. In her dark wood of error she questions God's Providence, revealing doubt of his Goodness, and thus follows in the footsteps of previous poets and scholars who have similarly questioned God, including Boethius (early sixth century) and Dante (early fourteenth century):

> To the best of my knowledge, no matter how long I confronted or dissected the problem, I could not see or realize how their claims could be true when compared to the natural behavior and character of women. Yet I still argued vehemently against

women, saying that it would be impossible that so many famous men—such solemn scholars, possessed of such deep and great understanding, so clear-sighted in all things, as it seemed—could have spoken falsely on so many occasions that I could hardly find a book on morals where, even before I had read it in its entirety, I did not find several chapters or certain sections attacking women, no matter who the author was. This reason alone, in short, made me conclude that, although my intellect did not perceive my own great faults and, likewise, those of other women because of its simpleness and ignorance, it was however truly fitting that such was the case. And so I relied more on the judgment of others than on what I myself felt and knew. I was so transfixed in this line of thinking for such a long time that it seemed as if I were in a stupor. Like a gushing fountain, a series of authorities, whom I recalled one after another, came to mind, along with their opinions on this topic. And I finally decided that God formed a vile creature when He made woman, and I wondered how such a worthy artisan could have deigned to make such an abominable work which, from what they say, is the vessel as well as the refuge and abode of every evil and vice. As I was thinking this, a great unhappiness and sadness welled up in my heart, for I detested myself and the entire feminine sex, as though we were monstrosities in nature. (Richards, pp. 3-5.)

Fortunately, just as Lady Philosophy consoles the despairing Boethius in the *De consolatione Philosophiae* (*The Consolation of Philosophy*), and just as Virgil aids the suicidal Dante in the *Inferno*, so also three ladies—Reason, Righteousness, and Justice, each with a different goal—console Christine by adducing examples of women warriors, queens, and inventors (Reason), chaste, loving, prudent women (Righteousness), and holy women (Justice). They belong to an allegorical city of women analogous to the Augustinian City of God and counter to the earthly city of man founded by homicidal Cain. The city they construct of such strong foundations and walls also counters the image of the walled garden of courtly love in which Jean's Herculean Lover takes his pleasure. At the end of her work Christine interprets the city as a defensive castle—"the refuge for you all, that is, for virtuous women, but also the defense and guard against your enemies and assailants, if you guard it well. For you can see that the substance with which it is made is entirely of virtue, so resplendent that you may see yourselves mirrored in it, especially in the roofs built in the last part as well as in the other parts which concern you" (Richards, p. 254). To the three traditional medieval classes of women—wives, virgins, and widows—Christine offers at the end practical strategies: wives should endure bad husbands and try to "moderate their vices," virgins should "be armed with the strength of virtue against the tricks of the deceptive," and widows should be pious, prudent, patient, strong, humble, and charitable in deeds and speech. Christine's ultimate advice to women is to avoid the Ovidian traps set by cunning men, in an inversion of that advice offered by Ovid's Duenna and Jean's Old Woman: "see how these men accuse you of so many vices in everything. Make liars of them all by showing forth your virtue, and prove their attacks false by acting well.... Oh my ladies, flee, flee the foolish love they urge on you!... Remember, dear ladies, how these men call you frail, unserious, and easily influenced but yet try hard, using all kinds of strange and deceptive tricks, to catch you, just as one lays traps for wild animals" (Richards, p. 256). Christine strips away the mask of the Old Woman so that she may counsel women to act virtuously and prudently and thereby resist wicked men, both in *Book of the City of Ladies* and in *Letter of Othea*.

In short, Christine's answer to the antifeminism of the scholastic and mythographic tradition is to reread the appropriate texts and then rewrite the tradition. If we select just one female figure found in Ovid's *Heroides*, Jean de Meun's *Romance*, Boccaccio's *De claris mulieribus (Concerning Famous Women)*, Chaucer's *Legend*, and Christine's *City of Ladies* and *Letter*—say, Dido—we can appreciate how polysemous, or multi-layered, that interpretation of the text can be, depending on the point of view from which it is read. And both positive (*in bono*) and negative (*in malo*) readings of Dido grew out of glosses and commentaries of the Middle Ages, depending on which classical work was being read. From the sympathetic perspective of Ovid's *Heroides*—a work about women heroes who suffer because of men—comes the view of Dido as a basically good woman deceived by tricky Aeneas; this view also appears in Chaucer's legend of Dido. From the point of view of her lover Aeneas, however—and Virgil's *Aeneid* is after all written from a point of view sympathetic to him—she is ruled by passions, as witnessed in her suicide after Aeneas leaves her. In the Middle Ages, when male poets incorporate the more positive Ovidian assessment of Dido into their works, they nevertheless depict her as a helpless and passive victim, as in this passage spoken by the Old Woman in Jean de Meun's continuation of the *Romance of the Rose* and echoed by Boccaccio in his *Concerning Famous Women* and Chaucer in his *Legend of Good Women*:

> No woman can come to a good end. Dido, the queen of
> Carthage, could not hold Aeneas, no matter how much she
> had done for him;.... To obtain his love, she gave him her city,
> her body, her possessions; and he so reassured her in turn that
> he promised and swore to her that he was and would forever
> be hers and would never leave her. She, however, had no joy
> of him, for the betrayer, without permission, fled by sea in his

ships. As a result, the beautiful Dido lost her life. Before the second day, she killed herself in her chamber with the sword that he had given her in her own hand. Remembering her lover and seeing that she had lost her love, she took the sword, quite naked, raised it point upward and placed it under her two breasts, then let herself fall on it. It was a great pity to see, whoever saw her do such a deed. He would have been a hard man who was not touched by pity when he thus saw the beautiful Dido on the point of the blade. Her sorrow over him who tricked her was so great that she fixed the blade within her body. (Dahlberg, ll. 13173-13210, p. 228.)

In contrast, Christine's sympathetic treatment of Dido in *City of Ladies* 1.46.1 emphasizes the queen's perspicacity and omits Aeneas almost entirely. Revealed as a clever woman who deceives her homicidal brother by throwing what he imagines to be treasure out of her boat as she escapes, she wins the African land on which to build Carthage by means of a ruse. Claiming only as much of the land on the beach as one piece of cowhide might enclose for a lodging, she then cuts the hide into narrow strips which together form one long, single strip that encloses the entire port area. Thereafter, ingenious Dido, as the first queen of Carthage, rules effectively and prudently. Her name, says Christine, reflects the real identity of this woman as a colonizer and adventurer, that is, in Latin a "virago," or a woman with a man's strength. Her relationship with Aeneas is minimized—unlike the focus on her episode of the *Aeneid* (Book Four) in most of the mythographies, on her disastrous liaison with Aeneas.

To return, then, to the "Quarrel of the Rose" with which we began this section, we might say that throughout the *Letter* and the *City*, Christine also rereads the *Romance*. Similarly inverting the literary prototypes which precede her work, Christine literally and figuratively substitutes, for the tricky Ovidian Duenna and the deceptively wise Old Woman of Jean de Meun, the truly wise goddess Pallas Athena (Minerva), who, as we shall later see, dominates both *Letter* and *City of Ladies*. Angry at the immoral use to which Jean de Meun puts his understanding of mythography and alarmed by his reification of the female, Christine rewrites the mythographic tradition to focus on the special and positive contribution of women to the history of civilization, specifically the nature of female wisdom and heroism. Her feminist euhemerism—a view of the gods as in fact originally worthy humans worshiped after death as divine—seems very modern in contrast to the old-fashioned misogyny dominating earlier mythographies and characteristic even of Boccaccio's learned work.

III. The Mythographic Tradition and the Medieval Genealogy of the Gods

Mythography, from "mythos," or "story," and "graphos," or "writing about," provides the earliest form of literary criticism in the West, although always associated with philosophy (in Greece) or with grammar (in Roman and medieval schools). The practice began with commentary on Homer's use of the gods in the *Iliad* and involved Stoic rationalization of Greek "lies" by means of allegorization of the gods into natural, moral, or historical categories. In the Middle Ages, mythography continued in the monastic and university schools because of the clerical need to learn Latin; glosses and commentaries proliferated to help with obscure and difficult allusions, many of which were mythological. The most favored texts for glossing early in the Middle Ages included Virgil's *Aeneid*, Statius's *Thebaid*, Lucan's *Pharsalia*, Boethius's *Consolation of Philosophy* and Martianus Capella's *De nuptiis Philologiae et Mercurii* (*The Marriage of Philology and Mercury*). Later in the Middle Ages two important works came to be used as schoolbooks, the anonymous *Ecloga Theoduli* (*The Eclogue of Theodulus*) and Ovid's *Metamorphoses*.

These two great segments of the tradition cover the early Middle Ages, 450-1250, and the later Middle Ages, 1250-1500. During the evolution of school exegesis of such texts, two important trends developed. First, beginning with Fulgentius and then the Merovingian period (sixth to the eighth century), mythological references from various sources began to be collected in handbooks and manuals, like those of the Vatican mythographers. Second, in the Carolingian and twelfth-century renaissances, the Christianity of the masters required reconciliation of "pagan" references and allusions in the texts and the older glosses with Christian morality, a reconciliation achieved by moralizing or Platonizing references to classical myth. Thus new works which invited this kind of extrapolation sprang up, like the *Eclogue of Theodulus* in the ninth century, with its parallels between biblical types and classical figures. In addition, new commentaries developed, often to aid the homilizing of the preaching friar outside the schools. In England in the fourteenth century, for example, commentaries on Augustine's *De civitate Dei* (*The City of God*) appeared, as did commentaries on Ovid's *Metamorphoses* in France. In Italy, where the commentary tradition took on a powerful secular and even chauvinistic turn, scholars glossed the national epic of the *Commedia* (*Comedy*) and developed extensive commentaries on the heroic figure of Hercules.

Because Christine was not educated in the schools, that is, educated in the most conventional way, her mythographic work, while in part indebted to earlier sources, was freer to react to the implicit (or explicit) tenets of the earlier tradition, often in rather amazing ways. She was, for example, the first writer in France to allude to or cite Dante, influenced by his work in her *Long Road of Learning* and parts of the *Mutation of Fortune.*⁵ Christine, born originally in Italy, is also indebted, in the *Letter of Othea* and to an extent in *City of Ladies*, to Boccaccio, Dante's successor as poet laureate and commentator (at least on the first few cantos of the *Inferno*). Her sources in the *Letter of Othea* have been identified as the *Ovid Moralized*, *Histoire ancienne jusqu'à César* (*Ancient History as far as Caesar*), the *Legenda aurea* (*Golden Legend*) of Jacobus Voragine, the *Manipulus florum* (*Handful of Flowers*) of Thomas Hibernicus, the *Dits moraux des philosophes* (*Moral Sayings of the Philosophers*), *Flores bibliorum* (*Flowers of the Bible*), Guillaume de Machaut's works, Dante's *Inferno*, and Boccaccio's *Concerning Famous Women*.⁶ Her sources in the *City of Ladies* also include the *Golden Legend* and Boccaccio's *Concerning Famous Women* and *Decameron*. Despite her lack of schooling, she was familiar with many contemporary works involving mythology and mythography. Indeed, one of her most original approaches in both the *Letter* and *City of Ladies* feminizes the medieval genealogy of the gods, used by Boccaccio as the structural premise of his *Genealogie deorum gentilium* (*Genealogy of the Gentile Gods*).

In the Middle Ages, genealogies of the gods were adapted to the moral and ethical purposes of the mythographers and their handbooks. Most anciently used by Hesiod in his *Theogony*, the genealogy served several purposes in the Middle Ages. First, as a mnemonic device, its rough structure allowed students of Latin reading the ancient epics to remember the relationships of the gods, given its additionally chronologically nature. Second, as a metaphor for the creation of the world it functioned as medieval cosmology or space physics, indicating how the world evolved out of separation of the waters above and below (Oceanus and Thetis) from the heavens (their son Caelus), which process resulted in progeny, represented by time (Saturn) and space, or nature (his sister Rhea), rulers of the first age, and their dark brother Phorcus.

From these elemental parents was born the created universe as we know it. The marriage of time and space (nature) engendered the four elements, represented by the four rulers of the regions of the world, Jupiter (fire), Juno (air), water (Neptune), and earth (Pluto), who were all seen as kin. From the four elements (and regions) were derived various continents

---

5   See Arturo Farinelli, "Dante nell'opere di Christine de Pisan," in *Aus Romanischen Sprachen und Literaturen Festschrift Heinrich Morf* (Halle: Niemeyer, 1905), pp. 117-52; see also Francesco Picco, *Damia di Francia e poeti d'Italia* (Turin: Lattes, 1921), on Dante and Christine.

6   From P. G. C. Campbell, *L'Épître d'Othéa: Étude sur les sources de Christine de Pisan* (Paris: Champion, 1924), esp. Section II, pp. 63-184. But other sources have been named: the *Chapelet des vertus* (*Chaplet of Virtues*), or *Fleurs de toutes vertus* (*Flowers of All Virtues*), among them. Sources for the *Letter* also include the *Assembly of Gods*, a fifteenth-century English work by John Lydgate.

and nations—Europe (the union of Jove-Europa), Troy (the union of Jove-Electra), Greece (the union of Jove-one of Atlantis's daughters), and Thebes (Cadmus founded it, in following his sister to Europa, although he married Hermione or Harmonia, the daughter of Venus and Mars). The planets, or the other gods, were defined by, and derived from, the relationships of the major gods: Saturn, father of Jupiter, was the oldest (farthest away from the earth), and was castrated by Jupiter (as he was said to have castrated his father Caelus). Venus sprang from the severed testicles of Saturn hurled into the ocean by Jupiter. From Jupiter and Latona came Apollo (sun) and Diana (moon). Jupiter's union with Maja produced Mercury, the messenger of the gods and the closest to earth after the moon. Only Mars lacks a genealogy.

Such lists or family trees, however, rarely appear explicitly in medieval mythographies, although they are implicit in the structure of many of the manuals. Genealogies appear in Hyginus 1-5, the first Vatican mythographer (Bode, p. 63), Paul of Perugia, Boccaccio, Forese da Donati, and Franceschino degli Albizzi.[7] Of these, Hyginus is a first-century mythography used extensively by the first Vatican mythographer (probably Adanan the Scot); Paul of Perugia and the others belong to the fourteenth century, along with Boccaccio. Some of these sources—especially the Boccaccio—were known to Christine, who deliberately repudiates the patriarchal technique of genealogical organization in her *Letter*.

One of the most important implications of Boccaccio's genealogical structure is its constitution of authority (Hyde, p. 742). The history of the universe in the Middle Ages begins with Genesis and the creation; if the gods are euhemerized—imagined as important men and women whose "temples" are in fact actual burial places—then contemporary poets are descended literally and metaphorically from the heroes and poets of a bygone era, the writers of the word descended from the Word. For Boccaccio, "The *Genealogy* owes its structure ultimately to the Bible. Its mythical generations, as recorded in the chapter headings and tables of rubrics, echo, and allude to, genealogical passages in the vulgate of both testaments.... In the ancient Hebrew, the same word, tōledōt, means both generation and history, so that the Bible passes on to Eusebius, Jerome, and their medieval followers an essentially genealogical mode of universal history" (Hyde, p. 742). By this we may understand patriarchal authority—the authority of the male line of inheritance, the passing of power from father to son.

In the medieval genealogies of the gods, the metaphor for cosmic creation is sexual intercourse, chiefly by the head god Jupiter or Jove. The

---

7 Thomas Hyde, "Boccaccio: The Genealogies of Myth," *PMLA*, 100 (1985), 737-45, here, p. 744n3.

joining of two different things—heaven and earth, male and female, soul and body—was necessary for the generation of new life, a *tertium quid* ("third thing") with its own identity, genes, name, and potency. Hence the family tree represented a genetic history, a metaphor for the cosmic chronology known as the history of the world—and the history of man. And the way in which Jupiter managed his sexual unions provided a moral base for the various nations (continents) such couplings engendered. A rape, an abduction, an incest, might result in progeny condemned to repeat the sins of the fathers, in this case, Jupiter, the father of us all and equivalent to Adam.

The fall of Adam and Eve, their eating of the fruit of the tree of knowledge of good and evil, and their expulsion from paradise catalyze the history of man and the birth of his redeemer, Christ. In pagan terms, human history begins with the adulteries of Jupiter, in that they culminate in the birth of Augustus Caesar, as in Ovid's *Metamorphoses*. In medieval terms, however, the adulteries of Jupiter explain national differences and lead to the kind of chauvinism that accompanied the birth of nations and the rise of the vernacular beginning in the twelfth century. Although the eighth-ninth century genealogy of the first Vatican mythographer, as tabulated and appended to this work, might seem anachronistic in this light, it will be enormously helpful to the student of Chaucer struggling with the network of mythological relationships in the *Troilus* or wondering over the pattern of the victimized women martyrs in the *Legend of Good Women*. It will also be enormously helpful to the reader of Christine's *Letter*, which attempted to elucidate and educate in related but transcendent ways.

Christine, like her near-contemporary Chaucer in England, deplored the chaos of the late fourteenth century, with its tumult caused by plague, One Hundred Years War, civil uprisings, peasants' revolt, famine, ice age, political strife, rising middle class, and breakdown of the authority of the church. It is no wonder that these late medieval poets turned to the mythologies of ancient Greece and Rome, repeated by the commentators and mythographers of the Middle Ages, for moral and political solutions to the pressing problems of their own age. The order and hierarchy they found in the patterns of mythological relationships firmly reestablished the primacy of virtue and vice, the efficacy of the Christian faith, the existence of a good God and a benevolent Providence.

Christine, ever sensitive to gender issues and seeing parallels between the ancient genealogical cycles and the present ruling families, emphasized the patriarchal bias of these histories to demonstrate the families' moral, political, and social failure: to her it was clear that the national genealogies, the heroic cycles, transmitted from father to son the seeds of their own destruction. Instead she offered a radical and innovative feminist mythography—the genealogy of the mother that would rebuild a new society. If Boccaccio the bastard used the legitimizing power of the genealogy to structure his major mythography, it may then seem no accident that his countrywoman Christine de Pizan feminized the same tradition—just as she retained her father's name and not her husband's.

If we examine more particularly the different cycles of myth conveniently summed up by the first Vatican mythographer in Myth 204, the preface to his third book, we will discover the flawed ancestry of the Trojans, the Greeks, the Thebans, so condemned to repeat their errors in their begetting of sons and daughters. Their flaws are flaws in leadership as well as morals. For this reason their nations are doomed—the sons and daughters die out. Only one line is preserved, holy, sanctioned, if we tease out the one hero who escapes his cousins' destiny and founds present-day France and present-day England—Aeneas's line. Virgil's hero, like Dante's later guide, as the son of Venus and Anchises (and nephew of Priam) escapes Troy to marry Lavinia, daughter of the king of Italy. His sons and grandsons will bear children who will found Rome, Britain, and other countries, as his ancestor Dardanus founded what was to become Florence, and as his uncle (or cousin) Antenor, traitor though he was, founded Padua (or Venice). Charlemagne, Holy Roman Emperor of the Franks, thus descended from Priam's son Hector through his son (or nephew) Francio; so also did Henry Plantagenet, through Arthur, from Brutus, eponymic founder of Britain and great grandson of Aeneas, according to Geoffrey of Monmouth writing in the twelfth century. Chaucer and Christine alike were accordingly fascinated by the story of Troy, promoting it both in poetic (*Troilus*) and didactic works (*Letter of Othea, Long Road of Study*). In the fall of Troy they read the auguries for their own nations and urged those warnings on to their nation's leaders.

We can first note that Troy is doomed because of its male ancestry, which is tainted by betrayal and deception. Jupiter treacherously overthrew his own father Saturn, a deceit that will echo in Laomedon's treacherous refusal, first, to pay Neptune, who had helped him build Troy's walls, and, later, Hercules. Laomedon is father of Antenor, who betrayed his country by allowing in the Trojan horse. He is also grandfather of Paris, who abducted Helen and initiated the Trojan War. Paris's decision, at the wedding of Peleus and Thetis, to choose as most beautiful of the three goddesses Juno, Venus, and Pallas, the goddess Venus, reflects this Trojan national problem of flawed judgment. Sent into the countryside to live in isolation as a baby (largely because his mother Hecuba dreams his existence will lead to his father's death and his country's downfall but because she is unwilling to kill him as her husband Priam has demanded), Paris has never known the love of a mother, or the love of a woman, until he meets—and betrays—the shepherdess Oenone. And in judging the three goddesses, the unmothered son therefore chooses Venus, who has promised him the love of the most beautiful woman in the world as a prize. In addition, because it was Discord who had thought up the idea of the contest when she threw the golden ball into the midst of the wedding guests, Discord appropropriately completes the story of Troy when the nation falls to the Greeks during the Trojan War just as the concept of discord has marked Saturn's fall from power at the hands of his own son. Hecuba, like Rhea, repeats the mistake of her husband's ancestor when she attempts to hide her son from Priam's wrath, as Rhea attempted to hide Jupiter from Saturn, who devoured all his sons except Jupiter.

The Greeks suffer similarly, disastrously, but from the unnatural (miscegenous, incestuous) sexual foibles of Jupiter, who sleeps with human women in the guise of various beasts, and whose wife Juno is his own sister. Jupiter was the great grandfather of Atreus, father of Agamemnon and Menelaus; he was also the father of Helen and Clytemnestra, sisters born from one of the two eggs produced from the rape of Leda by Jupiter in swan-form. The two sisters married the two brothers, avenging their mother's rape on their father by means of their life stories. Helen, who cuckolded Menelaus when she was raped (or abducted) by Paris, initiated the Trojan War. Clytemnestra, who consorts with Aegisthus in Agamemnon's absence and who murders her husband on his return from the war with Troy, is the mother of doomed and insane children, including the distraught Orestes, Ipighenia, a victim of her father's lust for battle and sacrificed by him to Diana to gain sailing winds, and the father-loving Electra. Atreus himself descended from a grandfather who sacrificed his child out of pride: Tantalus, to test the divinity of the gods, offered up his son Pelops as dinner to the visiting deities. Only Ceres bit into a shoulder, and for this error, brought Pelops back to life with an ivory replacement, while Tantalus was sent to hell.

Much later in the history of the Greek kings, we find parents sacrificing their children—out of ignorance, out of pride, or out of wrath. Pandion, father of the sisters Philomela and Procne, allows Philomela to leave with Tereus in order to join her married sister, but of course Tereus rapes and mutes her. When Procne discovers this incestuous and awful act, she serves up his son Itys to him at dinner. It is *his* son—the genealogies are traced patrilineally. The punishment fits the crime. So also Erechtheus, king of Athens after Pandion, produces two daughters, Procris and Orithyia, and with similar fates. Boreas rapes Orithyia, and jealous Cephalus mistakenly kills his wife Procris. Therefore, even though Agamemnon, Ulysses, and the other Greeks triumph over the Trojans by means of their cunning ruse of the Trojan horse—cunning also because of the Trojan predilection for and skill with horses—their cunning is worthless, a cold and heartless intellectual ability that, in its most degenerative form, will permit even the sacrifice of progeny to advance an end.

The Greeks will nevertheless also triumph over the Thebans, a nation more than any other suffering from division and self-destruction and therefore like the Trojans, unable to master themselves. Unlike the Trojans, however, the Thebans do not rape women, or deceive and betray their own kind. Their national sin, if one can term it so, is fatricide, self-destruction, disorder itself—the cosmic and familial equivalent of irrationality. The very site of Thebes and its origin signals its nature. Cadmus, following his sister Europa when she is abducted by Jove in the form of a bull, arrives in Boeotia, where he fights a terrible battle with a serpent. Advised by Minerva to sow the teeth of the serpent, Cadmus finds that they leap up as armed soldiers and destroy each other until only five (seven?) survive, who become the kings of Thebes. In the mythographies the serpent is cast as the devil and the kings as those who sow discord among brothers and who hate God. Indeed, Cadmus's daughters either self-destruct or kill their sons. During the festival of Bacchus (the god of the vine and celebrated by means of frenzied dancing, eroticism, and inebriation), Agave rips apart Pentheus; Semele demands that Jove make love to her in his own shape and is burned to a cinder; Autonoë's son Actaeon, after seeing Diana naked, is transformed into a stag and dismembered by his own dogs; Ino marries Athamas and watches her mad husband kill their children. Amphion, a later king, raises the walls of Thebes with his music but then marries Niobe, whose pride turns her to stone and kills her seven sons and seven daughters. All of them seem to deny or ignore the wisdom represented by the goddess Pallas Athena. Oedipus sleeps with his own mother, who produces two sons who kill each other during a civil war. At this point in the Theban history, Theseus of Athens quells the nation. Even so, later on Meleager, brother to Deianira, kills his uncles in a boar-hunt; in revenge, his mother ends his life. And his sister Deianira inadvertently kills her husband Hercules by means of a poisoned cloak that she sends him as a gift.

Christine was conscious of the doomed male bias in these national cycles. When she has to deal with the traditional genealogies, she reinterprets them. (Christine's Italian birth and ancestry probably motivated her in rewriting this genealogy.) For example, in many mythological histories Aeneas will, in part, escape his heritage because his father is Trojan Anchises, son of Laomedon, but his mother is a goddess—Venus, daughter of Saturn, god of time and associated with prudence in the later Middle Ages. Guided by her wisdom to Italy, he will avoid that self-indulgence characterizing the Trojans, in the view of the Italian poet-scholars Petrarch and Cristoforo Landino. Hence, his eventual arrival in Italy, where he will marry, carry on as king, and produce more children, marks the founding of the Empire for Dante, the creation of modern Italy and the home of Christianity. However, in Christine's *City of Ladies*, Saturnus is the ancestor of Lavinia, not just of Aeneas. In fact,

Aeneas is not mentioned at all. Lavinia's descendant Julius Silvius is the father of Romulus and Remus, but Christine fails to mention that Romulus founded Rome.

Her awareness of the failure of history is also reflected in the *City of Ladies*, in its attempt to reread and thus revise history by adding to it the successful women rulers and leaders that most such collections omit entirely or de-emphasize. In the first book—generally of greatest interest here because of its mythologizing—most pertinent are the stories of Hippolyta, Medea and Circe, Minerva, Ceres, Isis, and Arachne. She emphasizes the wisdom, prudence, and creativity of these women while ignoring their paganism. She prefers the qualities which contribute to their moral or rational strength as leaders or inventors. She also includes non-Greek and Roman women—Amazons, Egyptians, Babylonians, and Carthaginians—the conquered and non-European nations of Africa and the Middle East.

Thus, the advantage to Christine's lack of conventional schooling—as was also the case with the modern writer Virginia Woolf, with whom she has occasionally been compared—is her fresh and innovative approach to mythographic conventions. In her *Letter of Othea*, to which we shall now turn, her innovations result in what might be termed a gynocentric mythography.

IV. The *Letter of Othea* as a Mythographic Text

The *Letter* consists of one hundred verse texts describing a mythological figure or moment and prose moral glosses explaining how to read the myth in order to improve human character, followed by allegorical explanations. Its design, often criticized as eccentric or haphazard, overlays the fables with catalogues of the classical and Christian virtues, the sins, and the Twelve Articles of the Creed, linked with the Apostles and the Ten Commandments. Of the three different medieval levels, or senses, of allegory (a word meaning "other speaking," from the Greek), Christine uses only two in the *Letter*, in what Rosemond Tuve describes as a "double chivalry." For the first of the one hundred texts is a framing preface in which the goddess Othea addresses the fifteen-year old Trojan prince Hector.

Othea represents the mythical goddess of prudence, a mother to Hector in spirit if not in fact. She thus resembles Christine, who had a fifteen-year old son at the time this was written, and who is depicted in the accompanying manuscript illuminations in the identical pose as Othea when she hands her completed manuscript to Louis of Orleans. The name "Othea" probably derives from the Greek for "Goddess," used in the

Liturgy for Good Friday in the phrase "Agios o Theos," which might have been understood as "sanctus deus."[8] The gloss for this initial fable, however, explains that "O thea" "in Greek can be taken for the wisdom of woman," but also a real woman worshiped as a goddess, as was the practice at the time (indeed, "several wise women who existed at their time were called goddesses"). More specifically, Othea combines prudence and wisdom as reflected in the four cardinal virtues, which the knight should inculcate.

"Hector" was chosen for two reasons, most likely: as the classical exemplar of military prowess, he represents the prototype of the French chivalric hero in whom Christine remained interested her entire career; as the young hero, he nevertheless requires an education in virtue and wisdom, which "Othea" can ably supply. Second, the French kings traced their heritage back to the founding of Troy, as did the English kings. Hector represents the source of that founding line in terms of his epic prowess, if not his wisdom. The youthful dauphin might have been the same age as Hector at the time Christine presented her handsomely illustrated book.

Christine unifies and organizes her mythography by means of a reiteration of the wisdom and bravery—the *topos* (literary commonplace) of *sapientia et fortitudo*—which she believes the *chevalier*, or knight, should inculcate, and which the *miles Christi*, or warrior of Christ, in fact, does. This reiteration takes the form of a projection of the two qualities onto the two major figures involved in the framing prologue—Othea, termed the goddess of prudence in the opening lines of the framing text (1), or *sapientia*, who addresses the bachelor knight Hector (the youthful promise of *fortitudo*, or strength). Thus, Othea addresses the fifteen-year old Hector as the "noble and powerful prince," who "is ever flourishing in arms, / Son of Mars, the god of battle," and "of Minerva, the powerful / Goddess, who is mistress of arms" (lines 4-5, 7-8).

If Christine can be said to feminize valor and wisdom, she also subordinates the traditionally masculine heroic (Hercules) and powerful (Minos) to the dominant feminine "thea," the goddess. Following the introduction to Othea and Hector is a heroic series on the remaining cardinal (or classical) virtues, beginning with her sister, temperance or balance (2), strength (the Greek hero Hercules, 3), meaning not just bodily strength but "the constancy and firmness that the good knight ought to have in all of his deeds, resolved through good sense and strength," and justice (Minos, 4, judge of hell). All of these virtues are transported to heaven by good fame (the horse Pegasus, 5), ridden by the hero Perseus

8   See G. Mombello, "Recherches sur l'origine du nom de la Déesse Othea," *Atti della Accademia delle Scienze di Torino*, II, *Classe di Scienze Morali, Storiche e Filologiche*, 103 (1969), 343-75.

(in the same fable), who rescued Andromeda and who, with Minerva's aid, overcame the Gorgon. It is Perseus who incarnates all of the preceding virtues. In the Gloss, Othea explains that Perseus delivers Andromeda from the monster, as all knights should succor women who need them. Allegorically, the horse is Perseus's good angel and Andromeda his soul, which he rescues from the fiend. She means, then, that this wisdom and bravery must be used by the knight to battle the Adversary—the Antichrist. In the prologue to the allegory in the *Letter*, Christine has already explained that the good knight allegorically models himself upon Christ and fights the "enemy from hell," for, she declares, "we may call human life virtuous chivalry" (p. 37).

Having defined her heroic terms, Christine-Othea prepares to explain more specifically the virtues of the good knight by means of the seven planetary gods who, in their rule of the natural divisions of the cosmos, can be understood (with the exception of Venus and the moon, Phoebe) as representing translunary virtues. As qualities more than human, more than natural, they include in 6, Jove, prudence, or allegorically, mercy and compassion; 7, Venus, or lechery, vanity on the allegorical level, which the knight should avoid; 8, Saturn, careful judgment; 9, Apollo, truth; 10, Phoebe the moon, unsteadfastness or folly, which the knight should avoid; 11, Mars, valor, or the son of God which every good spirit should follow; 12, Mercury, eloquence, morally, "beautiful language adorned with rhetoric and with pontifical behavior," or, allegorically, "with good preaching and with words of doctrine."

Christine seems to link the first two series, the seven planetary gods and the seven deadly sins, by means of the moon, normally the last of the "planets" in the Ptolemaic universe and therefore morally lowest because of its proximity to the dense earth, material center of the universe, and its distance from spiritual lightness, the empyrean. The moon thus signifies the line of demarcation between the immutable translunary realm and the mutable sublunary realm in which we live on earth, subject to the vicissitudes of fortune. Also identified in classical mythology as the underworld, Hades, or the place to which the shades (*manes*) resorted after death, in Neoplatonic thought the region below the moon was understood as a moral underworld, a place where especially evil spirits were sent. Thus, the area from earth to moon came to symbolize the nature of earthly life (where moral choices governing the individual's afterlife are made) as hell, a place of concupiscence, desire, and evil.

According to Christine, the sublunary ideal in overcoming earthly temptation is reflected in Minerva (13), Pallas Athena (14), and Penthesilea (15), a specialized definition of the goddess Othea. That is, in between the series on the planetary gods (6-12) and the figures guilty of deadly sin (16-22), Christine inserts three female figures she views as reflective of the human ideal of chivalry (understood both literally and figuratively). In a sense, these three sum up aspects of Othea as faithful, wise, and strong—the perfect knight, and female, intent on battling the Adversary by means of virtue and good works.

Accordingly, Minerva suggests military strategy and cunning, as Pallas Athena represents wisdom, and the Amazonian Penthesilea combines both qualities in her desire, after Hector dies, to avenge his death by fighting against the Greeks. Minerva (13) assumes this significance because she is "a lady of very great wisdom and invented the art of armor-making, for previously the people did not arm themselves, except with *cuir boulu* [boiled leather]. And for the great knowledge which existed in this lady, they called her goddess." Pallas (14) seems very like Minerva, a goddess of wisdom called Pallas from the "island that has the name Pallence." Further, of the two names, the former

...is named Minerva in that which appertains to chivalry, and Pallas in all things which appertain to wisdom. And therefore it is said that he [the good knight] should unite wisdom to chivalry, which exists very well according thereto. And as weapons ought to be guarded, may be understood by faith; to this purpose Hermes says: "Join love of faith with wisdom." (14)

In both cases the Allegory appended to the Gloss suggests an interpretation of the myth based on Christ's (or the Christian's) life. For Minerva as armor-maker, Christine notes, the Christian virtue of faith is revealed: "And that she delivers enough armors, Cassiodorus says in the *Exposition on the Creed*, that faith is the light of the soul, the door of paradise, the window of life, and the foundation of everlasting health, for without faith no one can please God" (13). In addition, the joining of Pallas (wisdom) to Minerva (chivalry) means that hope should join faith: "And just as Pallas, who means wisdom, ought to be joined with chivalry, so also the virtue of hope ought to be joined with the good virtues of the chivalrous spirit, without the which he may not avail" (14).

As Christine has indicated at the beginning, human life can be understood as a vicious and miserable affair, with virtuous chivalry the only means of transcendence. Note, for example, the next series on the seven deadly sins, "moral" in that these sins are not revealed in the text of the fable but only in the Gloss on the text: Narcissus as pride (16), Ino/Juno as wrath (17), Aglauros as envy (18), Polyphemus as sloth (19), the men who do not aid Latona, avarice (20), Bacchus as gluttony (21), Pygmalion as lechery (22). Most interesting here is the equation of vice with male *figura* and de Pizan's careful omission of attribution of sin to female *figura* (for example, in the fable of Athamas and his queen, Ino). This means of unifying a narrative was used by Dante in the *Inferno* and the *Purgatorio*, both full of mythological examples, as well as John Gower in his *Confessio Amantis*, beginning with Narcissus as an example of pride.

There follows a series of *remedia*, remedies for those vices, all related to the Christian faith. In the Allegory for these fables, Christine uses the twelve Apostles linked with the twelve Articles of the Creed (the Credo, or Profession of the Faith) in 23-34, followed by the Ten Commandments. In most of these fables, the Apostles (and the Articles of Faith) are linked positively with female mythological figures. They begin with a female trinity most unusual for this time: initially Diana (23), the moon or chastity, represents God and relates to the first Article, introduced by St. Peter: "I believe in God the Father omnipotent, creator of heaven and earth." She is followed by Ceres (24), the goddess of corn, or liberality, as the Son of God; St. John introduces the second Article of the faith, "and in Jesus Christ, his only begotten son, our Lord." Isis (25), the goddess of plants and grasses, or the multiplication of virtues, rather remarkably signifies the Holy Ghost; St. James the Greater offers the third Article, "who is conceived by the Holy Ghost, is born of the Virgin Mary."

The other nine Apostles introduce a mixture of negative and positive classical figures—fools and heroes—in their association with the remaining articles of the Creed. Midas (26) signifies "little understanding," or a fool, a type of Pilate, and hence the fourth Article, according to St. Andrew ("passed before Pontius Pilate, was crucified, died, and buried"). Hercules's heroic descent into hell (27) to help his friends Theseus and Pirothosus, who wished to rescue Proserpina from Pluto, is imagined as like that descent of Christ to harrow hell and thereby to rescue the patriarchs and prophets from limbo (Article Five, "he descended into hell," according to St. Philip). Cadmus (28), founder of Thebes, defeated the serpent at the well (that is, cunning and wisdom, as the blessed manhood of Christ triumphs over life in this world, according to St. Thomas, touting the sixth Article ("On the third day he rose from the dead"). Cadmus's sister, Io (29), as the cow of sweet and nourishing milk, is interpreted as the letters and scriptures and stories of good people, or allegorically the good spirit that delights in Holy Writ (according to St. Bartholomew, Article Seven, "He ascended up to heaven, he sat at the right hand of God the Father omnipotent"). Her guard Argus is sung to sleep by Mercury (30), which the good knight should avoid because of the danger of being robbed; allegorically, sleep means incredulity of faith. Here St. Matthew reminds us, in Article Eight, that "he will come to judge the living and the dead."

Turning to the Trojan War, Christine includes Pyrrhus (31, Achilles's son) who avenged his father's death; so also the Holy Ghost is like, and proceeds from, the Father, according to St. James the Lesser, in Article Nine, "I believe in the Holy Ghost." Paris's sister Cassandra (32) speaks the truth and serves the gods, like the knight who should worship the Church and its ministers, allegorically like the good spirit in its devotion to Holy Church, according to St. Symond, in Article Ten, a "holy catholic church, a communion of saints." Neptune (33), god of the sea, keeps tempests away if his feast-day is observed, as the knight should serve God and his saints through words (prayers) and deeds, or the good spirit calling devoutly upon his maker to remit his sins, according to St. Jude, "the remission of sins," Article Eleven. For the last Apostle, and Article, Christine provides a masculine Atropos (34), death, the fear of which should propel the good knight to a virtuous life, as in the Passion of Christ, according to St. Matthew, "the resurrection of the flesh, eternal life."

The next series (35-44) links mythological figures with the Ten Commandments (from Exodus 20). The First Commandment appears in the fable of Bellerophon (35), whom Christine confuses with Hippolytus, is loved too much by his stepmother, and dies rather than succumb to her; allegorically he resembles God in heaven, in illustration of the Commandment (echoed in Matthew 4:10) that "Thou shalt not have strange gods before me." The Second Commandment appears in the fable of Memnon (36), who aids his cousin Hector in the Battle of Troy, avenges Hector's death by wounding Achilles, and reminds the knight to support his kin and the Christian to think of God of heaven who took on our humanity ("Thou shall not take the name of the Lord thy God in vain"). The Third Commandment is illustrated by the fable of Laomedon (37) who uses menacing words against Jason, Hercules, and the Argonauts, in contrast to the good knight, and therefore in contrast to the person who honors the Sabbath. The Fourth Commandment grows out of the tale of Pyramus (38), who in his presumption falsely assumes Thisbe's death, unlike the good knight, who should not grant too much importance to the insignificant sign; the fable reiterates, by antithesis, the commandment to "Honour thy father and thy mother, that thou mayest be longlived." For the Fifth Commandment, Aesculapius (39), who founded medicine, reminds the good knight to seek physicians and not enchanters (like Circe), and therefore embodies the Commandment, "Thou shalt not kill." To illustrate Commandment Six, in 40, Achilles mistakenly trusts Hecuba, whose children he had slain treacherously, and is then slain himself by Paris and his friends at the night meeting, thereby warning the good knight not to trust his enemies, or, more allegorically, to avoid evil, especially adultery. The Seventh Commandment is linked to the cruelty of Busiris to his guests (41)—he murders them—which is condemned as unnatural, reflective of the injunction not to steal (theft interpreted here as the taking of anything by force). For Commandment Eight, Leander's death while swimming the sea (Hellespont, 42) warns the knight not to love so much that he puts his life in danger, which also warns the soul not to bear false witness against his neighbor. The Ninth Commandment, not to covet your neighbor's wife, is illustrated in the fable of Helen (43), which reminds us to make peace instead of pursuing foolish debates. Finally, the last Commandment appears in the fable of Aurora (44), goddess of day, who changes her dead son Tynus into a swan, Cygnus, bewails his death her entire life, and therefore antithesizes the knight who should behave gladly and graciously before others. The good Christian, like the good knight, should not weep out of covetousness for worldly things, in reminder of the Tenth Commandment, "Thou shalt not covet thy neighbour's house: neither shalt thou desire...his servant, nor his handmaid, nor his ox, nor his ass, nor anything that is his."

After this series, the coherence of the collection only appears to break down (45-59). It offers fables, without any unifying pattern, on Pasiphae (45), Adrastus (46), Cupid (47), Coronis (48), Juno (49), Amphariaus (50), Saturn (51), Apollo's crow (52), Ganymedes (53), Jason (54), Gorgon (55), the discovery of Mars and Venus by Vulcan (56), Thamaris (57), Medea (58), Galatea (59).

Then, with the fable on Discord and the wedding of Peleus and Thetis (60), Christine initiates a long series predominantly covering the story of Troy, its founding and various falls, including the last one, at the hands of Ulysses and the Greeks, but also referring to the story of Thebes. The series includes the destruction of Laomedon, founder of Troy (61), Semele of Thebes (62), Diana as goddess of hunting, who hated Thebes (63), Arachne and Minerva (64), Adonis, son of Myrrha (65), the fall of the first Troy (66), Orpheus the (Theban) harper (67), the dream of Paris about Helen (68), Antaeus (69), Orpheus and Eurydice (70), Achilles and his mother Thetis (71), Atalanta (72), the Judgment of Paris (73), Fortune (74), Paris as lover, not warrior (75), Cephalus (76), Helenus, brother of Hector (77), Morpheus, god of dreams (78), Ceyx and Alcyone (79), Troilus (80), Calchas (81), Hermaphroditus (82), the playing of Ulysses (83), Criseyde (84), Patroclus and Achilles (85), Echo (86), Daphne and Apollo (87), Andromache (88), Babylon's capture by Minos (89), Hector's death (90), the discovery of Hector's arms (91), Polyboetes, slain by Hector (92), Achilles's love for Polyxena (93), Ajax (94), Antenor (95), Minerva's temple (96), Ilium (97), Circe and Ulysses's men (98), and Ino, wife of Athamas (99).

The reasons for Christine's interest in the stories of Troy and Thebes are similar to those for Chaucer's interest: the origin of France, like that of England, was traced back to Aeneas's founding of Italy, which occurred because he fled Troy before its fall. France's leadership thus descends from Charlemagne as Holy Roman Emperor. Given Christine's interest in peace during troubled times, the old stories, under cover of fable, gave valuable lessons to her courtly audience and patrons, especially those to whom she offered these expensive illuminated copies—King Charles VI, Louis, Duke of Orleans, Philip the Hardy, Duke of Burgundy, and Jean, Duke of Berry.

Christine took seriously her role as public poet, whatever the charges leveled against her Latin and Greek by scholars of her own (or later) times;

as a mythographer rewriting the tradition to provide the most humanistic education for her reader, she uses the classical tradition as catechism for the Church. The stretch and breadth of her intent is clear from the unifying devices of the Creed, the Liturgy, the Gospel. But, as if reminding her reader of the dangers in not reading carefully, she reintroduces a curious figure as her penultimate text. Ino, wife of Athamas (17), reappears in 99. The second wife of Athamas, Ino in 17 signifies the foolish stepmother who cut off her stepchildren from their inheritance, but in 99, more figuratively, the queen who sowed corn that never grew. The agricultural mistake is likened to presenting wise words to ignorant people—as if Christine were reminding herself of the danger of writing, as well as of reading. She then ends, in 100, with a fable about the prophetic and wise Sibyl, who, in fact, is responsible for the education and conversion of Caesar Augustus, who lived at the time of both Virgil and Christ. Christine's handbook thus ends as does Ovid's, with a tribute to, if not an apotheosis of, Caesar Augustus, a thinly disguised exemplar for her own king—and her own son.

Caesar is portrayed as emperor of the Romans and the world at a time when Christ also lived, a leader wisely converted to belief in Christ through the influence of the Othea-like Sibyl. Through her he gains a vision of the Virgin Mary and her Child. Christine means to imply that through Othea's own "didascalicon" Hector will "convert" and learn, as we all will learn through her: "There where Othea says that she has written to him one hundred authorities and that Augustus learned from a woman, is to understand that good words and good teaching bring praise to whichever persons have said them." To end her mythography, Christine refers to the third chapter of Ecclesiasticus, verse 31: "The heart of the wise is understood in wisdom, and a good ear will hear wisdom with all desire." It is no accident that Christine's last word is Latin, *sapiencia*, or wisdom, and that the agent of Caesar's education is, like the author of the *Letter*, a woman.

Prologue to the Letter of Othea

Most high flower praised by the world, [1]
    To all pleasing and by God protected,
Gentle delight, sweet smelling, charming,
Of great worth, notable above all others:
Praise to God before this work be sent   5
And then to you, noble flower who has been sent
From Heaven to ennoble the world, [2]
Nobility so righteous and pure, [3]
From the Trojan stock of ancient nobility,   10
Pillar of faith which no error blemishes,
Whose great renown can find nowhere to hide;
And to you, most noble and excellent prince,
Duke of Orleans, Louis of great renown,
Son of Charles, fifth king of that name,   15
Who, apart from the king, knows no one greater, [4]
My most praised and powerful lord:
From humble desire, I, poor creature,
Unschooled woman, of small stature,
Daughter of the former philosopher and doctor,   20
Who was counselor and humble servant
Of your father, may God have mercy upon him,
And who once came by his command, [5]
From Boulogne la Grace where he was born,
Master Tommaso de Pizan, once   25
Was called and named De Boulogne,
Who was renowned as a serious scholar,
Desiring, if I know enough, to fashion
A pleasing thing that might give you   30
Some pleasure, this would do me great honor.
For this enterprise, I have, from unworthy memory,

---

1   Isabeau of Bavaria, to whom this copy of the *Letter* was dedicated.
2   Hector.
3   As Loukopoulos points out, in the French, Christine often uses identical words with different meanings, thus making a "poor rhyme" (*rime pauvre*) (see Loukopoulos, 310). The example here is "Et puis a vous, noble fleur qui tramise / Fustes du ciel pour anoblir le *monde*, / Seigneurie tres droicturiere et *monde*, ..." Loukopoulos 150/8-10 (italics mine). The first *monde* is used as a noun meaning "world" and the second as an adjective meaning "pure." Other examples in the prologue include 150/22-23 where *grace* is used as "mercy" and in a place name; 152/18-19 where *digne* is used as "worthy" and as "endowed."
4   Louis, Duke of Orleans.
5   By the command of King Charles V.

In presenting this work in rhyme,
My fears, to send it to you
The first day on which the year renews itself;   35
For so much is the matter herein new,
Though it be of rude signification
For meditation (for I lack perceptivity
Of profound meaning), in this case I do not resemble
My good father, except as one who steals   40
Grains of wheat while gleaning during the harvest,
In the fields and near the woods;
Or crumbs falling from the high table
That one scrabbles to gather when the dishes are of note;
Nothing more have I gathered   45
From his great wisdom, from which he has greatly reaped.[1]
Thus if you please, do not scorn my work,
My powerful lord, kindly and wise,
For the contempt of my ignorant person,
Since the small bell often sounds a great voice,   50
Which, quite often, awakens the wisest
And counsels them to the labor of study.
For this, prince most praiseworthy and benign,
I, named Christine, woman unworthy,
Have acquired knowledge, in order to undertake such worthy work: 55
To rhyme and recount, I wish to take
A letter which was sent
To Hector of Troy, so history teaches us;
If it is not so, well may it be likely.
And in this, there will be many verses and many deeds,   60
Lovely to hear and better to study.
Henceforth I wish to present this beginning.
Now God gives to me, to sing his praises,
Each deed, saying, and thing which may please
You, my redoubted lord, for whom I undertake it[2]   65
And humbly I beg, if I err,
The generosity of your great nobility,
That you pardon me for this excessive audacity
In writing to you, a person so very worthy,
The undertaking of myself, in wisdom unworthy.   70

---

1   Note the agricultural and harvesting imagery, which Christine later emphasizes in her
    choice of models for Hector to emulate. Such imagery is also emphasized in *The
    Book of the City of Ladies.*
2   "It" refers to the "beginning."

In order that those who are neither clerics nor poets understand in the form of a letter the meaning of the stories in this book, it should be known that everywhere where there are images among clouds it is to be understood that these are the figures[1] of the gods or goddesses of whom the following book speaks according to the manner of the ancient poets. And in that deity is a thing spiritual and elevated above the earth; these are the images figuring in clouds and the first one is the goddess of wisdom.

Here begins the Letter of Othea the goddess which she sent to Hector of Troy when he was at the age of fifteen years.

1 Othea

Text

Othea, goddess of prudence
Who addresses hearts great in valor,
To you, Hector, noble and powerful prince,
Who is ever flourishing in arms,
Son of Mars, the god of battle, 5
Who carves out and wages feats of arms,[2]
And of Minerva, the powerful
Goddess, who is mistress of arms,
Successor of noble Trojans,
Heir of Troy and of its citizens 10
Salutation I put in front
With true affection, without pretense.
And as I desire
Your great profit, which I go seeking,
And that it be augmented and 15
Preserved, and at all times recognized,
May your valor and great prowess
Aid you in your prime Youth.
By my letter I wish to counsel
You, and to say and to exhort 20
Those things which are necessary
To great valor and contrary
To the opposite of prowess,
So that your good heart address itself
To acquiring skillfully 25
The horse which takes flight in the air,

---

1 By "figures" Christine here means the miniature paintings preceding each chapter.
2 *Taille*, "carves out," can also mean "cuts to pieces."

That is, Pegasus the renowned,
Who is loved by all the valiant.
In that I know, by virtuous
Propensity, your condition,[1]   30
In chivalrous feats you are more
Adept than a hundred thousand others,
And as goddess I know
By science, not trial and error,
The things which are to come,   35
It remains to me to remind you,
As I know that always you will be
The most expert of all the expert and will have
Above all other others renown,
Provided that I be loved by you.   40
Loved, and why should I not be?
I am she who counsels all
Those who love and hold me dear.
I read to them their lessons in chair,[2]
Which enables them to mount to heaven.   45
Thus I pray that you be among them
And that you truly believe in me.
Now put it well into your memory
The deeds that I wish to describe to you.
And if you dare to recount or say to me   50
Something which is to come to pass,
Then I say to you that souvenirs[3]
Are your right as if they were past;
Know that they are in my thoughts
In the spirit of prophecy.   55
Now listen and do not worry yourself,
For I shall say nothing that will not come to pass;
If it does not happen, then you will remember it.

Gloss

Othea in Greek can be taken for the wisdom of woman, and as the
ancients, not yet possessing the light of true faith, idolized several gods,
under whose law passed the noblest lordships which have existed in the
world, such as the kingdom of Assyria, of Persia, the Greeks, the Trojans,

---

1 Hector's social position.
2 That is, Othea gives lessons to those who love her while she is seated. The chair is a
   symbol of authority. Note that Christine assigns the role of an educator to a female
   figure.
3 That is, those deeds being remembered: Christine is here grappling with the problem
   of Othea's foreknowledge of events that will occur during Hector's maturity—yet to
   come if he is now fifteen.

Alexander, the Romans, and many others and even the greatest philosophers, as God had not yet opened the door of his mercy. At the present time, we Christians, by the grace of God enlightened with true faith, are able to restore to morality the opinions of the ancients, and on these, many excellent allegories can be made.

And as these ancients had the custom of embellishing all things which out of the common course of things current took precedence over any grace, several wise women who existed at their time were called goddesses. And it is true, according to history, that in the time when great Troy flourished amid such high renown, a very wise woman, named Othea, considering the beautiful youth of Hector of Troy, who already flourished in virtues which could be demonstration of the graces to exist in him in the time to come, sent to him several beautiful and notable gifts, and particularly the handsome steed called Galathea, who had no equal in the world. And because all earthly graces that the good must possess existed in Hector, we can say morally that he acquired them by the counsel of Othea, who sent this letter to him. By "Othea" we take to signify the virtue of prudence and wisdom, with which he himself was adorned. And as the four cardinal virtues are necessary to good policy, we shall discuss that in the following. And to the first virtue we have given the name, and taken the manner of speaking, in part poetically and according to the true history, to better follow our subject, and to our end we take as some authorities the ancient philosophers. Thus we shall say that by the aforementioned lady was folded and sent this gift to the good Hector, who as example may serve to all others desiring goodness and wisdom. And as the virtue of prudence is much to be recommended, so declares the prince of philosophers, Aristotle: "In that knowledge is the most noble of all other things, it must be demonstrated by the best reasoning and in the most appropriate manner."

Prologue to the Allegory

To return the subject of our discussion to allegory, let us apply the Holy Scripture to our saying for the edification of the soul of this miserable world.

As by the great knowledge and high power of God all things are created, rationally so must all things lead at the end to him, and because our spirit, which God created in his image, is of the things created the most noble after the angels, an appropriate thing it is and necessary that it be adorned with virtues by means of which it may be guided to the end for which it was fashioned. And in that it [the spirit] may be hindered by the ambushes and assaults of the enemy from hell, who is its mortal adversary and often turns it away from the attainment of its beatitude, we may call human life virtuous chivalry, as the Scripture says in several places. And as all terrestrial things are fallible, we must have in continual memory the future time which is without end. And in that it is the great and perfect chivalry, and all else is of no comparison, and for which the victorious will be crowned in glory, we will take the manner of speaking of the chivalrous spirit; and this be done for the praise of God principally and for the profit of those who will read this present treatise.

Allegory

As prudence and wisdom are mother and conductress of all virtues, without which the others could not be well governed, it is necessary to the chivalrous spirit that it be adorned with prudence, as says St. Augustine in the book on *The Singularity of Clerics,*[1] that, wherever prudence is found, one can easily end and vanquish contrary things; but where prudence is scorned, all things contrary have lordship. And to this end speaks Solomon in Proverbs: "If wisdom shall enter into thy heart, and knowledge please thy soul: counsel shall keep thee, and prudence shall preserve thee." Proverbs 2[10:11]

Temperance was also called goddess, and because of this our human body is composed of diverse things and must be tempered: according to reason, it can be symbolized as a clock, which has several wheels and weights, and always the clock is worth nothing if not regulated; similarly our human body does not work if temperance does not regulate it.[2]

2 Temperance

Text

And to this end, that you may know
What you should do, that you know
In yourself the virtues more propitious
The better to reach the premises
Of chivalrous valor,   5
And however reckless it may be,
Again I shall tell you who dwells with me:
I have a first cousin of mine,
Full of all beauty;
But above all, especially   10
She is sweet, soft, and well-balanced;
She is never shaken by ire for any length of time;
She never thinks without measure;
This is the goddess of temperance.

---

1   Christine's primary source for citations from the Church Fathers was the *Manipulus florum* of Thomas Hibernicus.

2   The body, to remain healthy, must have in balance the four humors or fluids, blood, phlegm, yellow and black bile. An excess of any one, brought on by too much eating or drinking, physical pleasure, etc., was believed to cause imbalance, or illness. This passage does not appear in all manuscripts.

If you may not have the name   15
Of great grace named itself through her,
For if she would have little weight for you,
You would not even be worth a pea.
Therefore I would that with me she love you;
That this may be, let her not be forgotten.   20
For this is a very learned goddess,
Whose wisdom is much loved and valued.

Gloss

Othea says that temperance is her sister, whom he [the knight] ought
to love. The virtue of temperance truly may be called sister and resembling
prudence, for temperance is demonstration of prudence and from
prudence itself follows temperance. For this indicates that he takes her for
his friend, from which resemblance ought to make all good knights desire
the reward due to the good. As the philosopher named Democritus says:
"Temperance moderates the vices and perfects the virtues."

Allegory

The good spirit ought to possess the virtue of temperance, which has
the property of limiting things. And St. Augustine says in the book on *The
Conditions of the Church* that the office of temperance is to refrain and
appease the conditions of concupiscence, which make difficulties for us
and which turn us away from the law of God, and also to despise carnal
delights and worldly praise. To this purpose St. Peter speaks in his first
Letter: "I beseech you as strangers and pilgrims, to refrain yourselves from
carnal desires which war against the soul." 1 Peter 2[:11] [1]

3 Hercules

Text

And among us strength is necessary for you:
If you set store by great virtue,
Toward Hercules you ought to turn
And gaze at his worthiness—   .
A figure in whom there was much valor.   5
And for all that he was contrary
And bore animosity toward your lineage,[2]
Do not for all that have greater hate
For his noble and strong virtues,
Which have opened the doors of prowess.   10
But if you would like to follow them
Just for his valor to be continued,

---

1 Christine's major source for citations from the Bible was the *Flores Bibliorum*.
2 Hercules bore animosity toward Laomedon, founder of Troy and ancestor of Hector,
because the latter refused to pay him for his help as promised.

It is not at all necessary for you
To make war on the shades,
Nor to journey to contest with the god Pluto   15
To intend to have Proserpina,
The daughter of Ceres the goddess,
Whom he ravished on the sea of Greece.
Nor is it any mystery to you
How you cut the chains   20
From Cerberus, the porter of hell,
Nor how to take from hell those most adverse,
Who are excessively disloyal mastiffs,
As he did for his companions,
Pirotheus and Theseus,   25
Who almost were deceived
Into plunging into that valley
Where many a soul is greatly aggrieved.
You will find war enough on earth
Without going to hell to find it.   30
So it is not at all necessary to you
To acquire arms and make
A journey to battle with fierce serpents,
Or lions, or rampaging boars
(I do not know whether you imagine this),   35
Or else other serpentine things,
In order to have renown for prowess,
If there be no such danger
As in defending your body;
If such beasts in order to offend you   40
Assail you, then defense
Is honorable to you, and without doubt
If you have victory over them,
There will be honor and glory for you.

Gloss

The virtue of strength is to understand not only physical strength, but constancy and firmness that the good knight ought to have in all his deeds, resolved through good sense and strength to resist the contrary things which can happen to him, be they misfortunes or tribulations, where a strong and powerful spirit may be valuable in the exercise of valor. And in order to give a material example of strength, note Hercules, to the extent that it may be doubly valuable; that is to say, in all that touches this virtue and especially in deeds of chivalry, wherein he was most excellent. And given the eminence of Hector, it may be a suitable thing to give him a noble example. Hercules was a knight of Greece of marvelous strength, and brought to an end many a chivalric proceeding. A great voyager he was throughout the world, and for the great and marvelous actions, voyages, and things of great strength which he performed, the poets, who speak under *couverture* [cover] and in the manner of fable, said that he went to hell to fight with the infernal princes and so that he might fight with serpents and fierce beasts, which is to understand the brave enterprises that he might perform. And therefore this indicates to the good knight that he ought to look carefully: that is to understand, in these proceedings and valiant deeds, according to his ability. And just as the clarity of the sun is profitable to all may be a good example. And as a philosopher says: "The grain of wheat, when it falls in good earth, is profitable to everyone." Similarly, a good example may be valuable to all those who desire valor, and therefore a wise man says: "The virtue of strength makes man abiding and able to overcome all things."

Allegory
Just as, without strength and vigor, the good knight may not deserve the prize in arms, so also the good spirit may not, without it, have or win the reward due to the good ones. And St. Ambrose says in the first book of *The Offices* that the true strength of human courage is that which is never broken in adversity and never puffed up in prosperity; which attempts itself to guard and defend the adornments of the virtues and to sustain justice; which is hardy in perils and unyielding against carnal desires. And to this purpose St. John the Evangelist speaks in his first Epistle: "I write unto you, young men, because you are strong, and the word of God abideth in you, and you have overcome the wicked one." 1 Peter 2[:14][1]

4 Minos

Text
Again, if you wish to be one of us,
It behooves you to resemble Minos,
Though he be judge and master
Of hell and of all its environs.
For if you would advance,
It is necessary for you to be a judge.
Otherwise you are not worthy
To wear a helmet, or govern a realm.

Gloss
Prudence says to the good knight that if he wishes to be of a good rank, it behooves him to have the virtue of justice, that is to say, to hold righteous justice. And Aristotle says: "He who is a righteous judge ought first to judge his own self, for he who would falsely judge his own self would not

---

1   It should be 1 John 2[:14].

be worthy of judging another." This is to understand how to correct his own faults, so that they be wholly abated, and then a man may well be so corrected, and ought to correct other men. And to speak morally, we shall tell a fable to this purpose in accord with the cover[1] of the poets. Minos, so the poets declare, a judge of hell, as if one might say a provost or bailiff, and before him are amassed all the souls descending into this same valley; and after they have been designated a penance, and according to the degrees he wishes that they be sent to a particular depth, he twists his tail about him.[2] And because hell is the justice or punishment of God, let us take rendering justice in the present manner of speaking to our purpose especially this part. And the truth was that in Crete of old there was a king named Minos of marvelous pride, and he had in him great severity of justice. And therefore the poets declare that after his death he was commissioned to be judge of hell. And Aristotle says: "Justice is a measure that God has established on earth as a limit on things."

Allegory

And as God is chief of justice and of all order, it is necessary for the chivalrous spirit arriving at glorious victory that he have this virtue. And St. Bernard says in a sermon that justice is no other thing but to render to each that which is his. "Render," says he, "therefore, to the three kinds of people that which is theirs: to your sovereign, reverence and obeisance, reverence of heart and obeisance of body; to your equal you ought to render counsel and aid in instructing his ignorance and aid in comforting his weakness; to your subject you should render guarding and discipline, guarding in guarding against evil doing and discipline in chastising him when he has done evil." To this purpose Solomon speaks in the Proverbs: "The just considereth seriously the house of the wicked, that he may withdraw the wicked from evil. ... It is a joy to the just to do judgment." Proverbs 21[:12,15]

5 Perseus

Text

After, gaze on Perseus,
Of whom the high name is known
Throughout the world in all parts.
Pegasus the able horse
He rode through the air in flying,[3]   5
And in traveling he rescued

---

1 *Couverture.*
2 The tail of Minos acts as a kind of spearhead shooting the sinner down to the appropriate circle of hell. Dante's description in *Inferno* 5 aptly demonstrates what Christine means here.
3 Actually Bellerophon rode Pegasus. However, Pegasus was born of Medusa's blood after she was beheaded by Perseus.

Andromeda from the sea monster
And has taken [her] away by force;
Like the good knight errant
He has returned her to her parents.   10
This deed you might wish to remember,
For the good knight ought to hold
This view if he would have
Honor, which he values much more than riches.
Then gaze in his shining   15
Shield, which has overcome several.[1]
Be armed with his sword,
So that you will be strong and steadfast.

Gloss

And because it is an appropriate thing that a good knight is due honor
and reverence, we shall create a figure[2] according to the manner of the
poets. Perseus was a very valiant knight and he acquired several realms,
and from him was the great country of Persia named. And the poets declare
that he rode the horse which flew through the air. He bore in his hand a
sword or a scythe, which is said for the great plenty of the peoples which
through him were vanquished in various battles. He delivered Andromeda
from the sea monster. This was a maiden, daughter of the king, [whom he
delivered] from a monster of the sea which through the wisdom of the
gods should have devoured her, which is to understand that all knights
ought to succor women who have need of their aid. So may be understood
Perseus and the horse who flies as the good fame which the good knight
ought to have and acquire through these good merits; and he ought to ride
horseback, that is, his name ought to be carried into all countries. And
Aristotle says: "Good fame makes a man dazzling to the world and
agreeable in the presence of princes."

Allegory

The chivalrous spirit should desire celebrity within the company of
the saints of Paradise, acquired through his good merits. The horse
Pegasus who carries him will be his good angel, who will make good
account of him on the day of judgment. Andromeda who will be rescued,
it is his soul that he will rescue from the enemy of hell through mastery
of sin. And that one ought also to wish to have good fame in this world
for the pleasure of God, not through vainglory, St. Augustine in the *Book
of Correction* indicates that two things are necessary to live well, that is
to say, good conscience and good reputation, conscience for himself and
reputation for his neighbor, and whoever trusts in conscience and despises

1 Specifically, it allows Perseus to overcome Medusa (in Fable 55) when he gazes at
  her image reflected in the shield and is thus not petrified by her.
2 Figure, meaning figure, form, or shape and conveying the idea of fiction, veil, mask.

reputation, he is cruel; for it is a sign of noble courage to respect the good of reputation. And to this purpose the sage declares: "Take care of a good name: for this shall continue with thee, more than a thousand treasures precious." Ecclesiasticus 41[:15]

And it is to know that because of the seven planets in the heavens turning by the revolution of the sphere that one names the zodiac, the images of the seven planets are here figured seated on the spheres. And because they are seated in the firmament and on the upper side of the clouds, they are in these portraits stellified in the heavens on the upper side of the clouds. And of old they were called the great gods. And because Jupiter is a planet in the heavens which gives influence of sweetness and friendship, this image offers in sign of love his hand to men on earth. And because the dew of the heavens is cause of fertility and abundance, and the sweet-tempered air comes from this planet, he is here portrayed casting dew against the vale.[1]

6 Jupiter

Text
And with your inclinations
Look to have Jove's
Conditions; you would become better
If you would tender them to the right degree.[2]

Gloss
As it is said, the poets, who adored various gods, held the planets of the heavens as especial gods and from the seven planets they took the seven days of the week. Jupiter or Jove they adored and held for their greatest god, because he is seated in the highest sphere of the planets below Saturn. From "Jove" the day of *jeudi* [Thursday] is named. And similarly the philosopher attributed and compared the seven metals to the seven planets and named the terms of their sciences by the same planets, as one may see in Geber and Nicolas[3] and the other authors of that science. To Jove they attribute copper or brass.[4] Jove or Jupiter is a planet of sweet condition, amiable and joyful, and is figured with a sanguine complexion. For this declares Othea, that is to say, prudence, that the good knight should have the conditions of Jupiter. And all the nobles pursuing chivalry ought to have the same. To this purpose Pythagoras says that a king ought

---

1 This paragraph on the planets appears only in Harley 4431.
2 Christine is here referring to astrological "inclinations" and angles which produce certain "conditions" in humans. She is also punning on "tender," given Jove's softness.
3 "Geber" is Arabian—Jābir ibn Haiyān; "Nicolas" may be Nicolas de Farnham or Nicholas of Lynne.
4 Normally his metal is tin.

graciously to converse with his people and show them a joyful face, and through this also is to understand of all valiant ones tending to honor.

Allegory

Now let us recall to allegory our purpose, the properties of the seven planets. Jupiter, which is a planet sweet and human, of which the good knight should have conditions, we may signify mercy and compassion that the good knight, Jesus Christ, that is, the spirit, should have in himself. For St. Gregory in the Letter to Nepocian says: "I do not remember," says he, "having read or heard that he was dead of an evil death who has willingly accomplished the works of mercy, for mercy has many intercessors and it is impossible that the prayers of many will be exhausted." To this purpose speaks our Lord in the Gospel:"Blessed are the merciful: for they shall obtain mercy." Matthew 5[:7]

Venus is a planet in the heavens that the pagans of old named goddess of love, because she gives influence of being amorous; and for this reason lovers are here figured who present to her their hearts.[1]

7 Venus

Text
Do not make Venus your goddess,
Do not set store in her promise.
The pursuit of her is painful,
Not honorable, and perilous.

Gloss
Venus is a planet in the heavens, after whom the day of Friday[2] is named; and her metal which we call tin or pewter[3] is attributed to her. Venus gives influence of love and of idleness; and she was a lady so named who was the queen of Cyprus. And because she exceeded all in excellent beauty and voluptuousness, and was very amorous and not constant in one love but abandoned to many, they called her the goddess of love. And for this reason, that she gave influence of lechery, Othea says to the good knight that he not make her his goddess. This is to understand that, in this life which promotes vices, he should not abandon his body nor his intent. And Hermes says: "The vice of lechery taints all virtues."

Allegory
Venus, whom the good spirit should not make his goddess, signifies that the good spirit ought not to have in himself any vanity. And Cassiodorus says on the Psalms: "Vanity makes the angel become a devil; and gave death to the first man, and separated him from the blessedness that

---

1 The description refers to accompanying manuscript illuminations.
2 *Vendredi* in French.
3 Copper is her metal in the mythographies.

had been accorded to him. Vanity is mother of all evils, the fountain of all vices and the vein of iniquity which places man beyond the grace of God and sets him in his hate." To this purpose David in his Psalter says in speaking to God: "Thou has hated them that regard vanities." Psalm 30[:7]

Saturn is a planet slow and heavy, and this can signify in each case wisdom and moderation and calm condition; and for this is he portrayed as an ancient man. And because in the firmament he is seated at the top of all the planets, he is by this figured as seated above the seven circles and on earth underneath him some lawyers and wise men who speak of wisdom together. He holds a sickle because this planet was named after a wise king who had the name Saturn, who invented the manner of cutting grain with scythes.[1]

8 Saturn[2]

Text
If you meet in judgment,
Saturn guards what you resemble;
Before you pronounce the sentence,
Watch that you do not give it in doubt.

Gloss
From "Saturn" the day Saturday is named, and the metal that we call lead, and is a planet of slow condition, heavy and wise. And there was a king in Crete thus named, who was very wise, of whom the poets spoke under cover [*couverture*] of fable; and they said that his son Jupiter cut off his genitals, which is to understand that he took from him the power that he had and disinherited and chased him away. And because Saturn is heavy and wise, Othea wishes to say that the good knight should weigh carefully the thing also that he gives as his wisdom, whether this be in prize of arms or some other affair. And all wise beings may note this same that has offices appertaining to judgment. And to this purpose says Hermes: "Think well on all your affairs, and most especially in judgment of another."

Allegory
As the good knight ought to be slow in judgment of another, that is to say, to consider well the sentence also that one gives him, so also should the good spirit of that which appertains to him; for to God appertains judgment, who knows how to discern the causes righteously. And St. Gregory says in his *Morals*[3] that when our fragility does not know how to comprehend the judgments of God, we must not discuss them in hard

---

1 This passage on Saturn does not appear in all manuscripts.
2 See also Fable 51.
3 *Moralia* 27.3, *PL* 76: 401-2.

words, but ought to honor them in fearful silence; and however marvelous that it seems to us, nevertheless we ought to hold them just. And to this purpose David speaks in the Psalter: "The fear of the Lord is holy, enduring for ever and ever: the judgments of the Lord are true, justified in themselves." Psalms 18[:10]

The sun, which in ancient times they named Phoebus or Apollo, is a planet which illumines or clarifies all things troubled and obscure, who signifies truth which clarifies all things troubled and clouded. And for this reason there is a people underneath who make the sign of swearing and make promise to speak truth.[1] *He [Apollo] holds a harp, which may be taken for the beautiful accord and sweet sound which exists in the virtue of truth; he has next to him a crow, which signifies the first age of the world, which was spotless and afterwards darkened through the sins of creatures.*[2]

9 Apollo

Text
Let your word be clear and true,
Apollo will give you memory of it,
For he cannot tolerate
Any filth under cover.[3]

Gloss
Apollo or Phoebus, that is, the sun, to whom the day of Sunday is attributed and also the metal which we call gold. The sun through its clarity reveals things hidden; and because truth is clear and reveals secret things, it can be attributed to him. The same virtue ought to exist in the heart and the mouth of each good knight. And to this purpose says Hermes: "Love God and truth, and give loyal counsel."

Allegory
Apollo, that is to say the sun, by which we know the truth, we may take that one ought to have in the mouth truth, the real knight Jesus Christ,[4] and must flee all falsity. As Cassiodorus says in the book of *The Praises of St. Paul:*[5] "The condition of falsity is such that, even where it has no

---

1 This refers to a manuscript illumination not in all manuscripts.
2 See Fable 48.
3 *Couverture*: Christine implies a disguise, dissimulation. Note that the twelfth-century term *integumentum*, used for pagan fable, means literally "covering," and in antiquity a platecover, or lid.
4 The Host. Note the reference to the Elevation of the Host below. Apollo was commonly identified as Christ in the mythographies.
5 The Latin text of *The Praises of St. Paul* belongs to Chrysostomus, not Cassiodorus.

naysayers, it falls from usage by itself; but, on the contrary the condition of truth is so firm that the more naysaying adversaries it has, the more is increases and elevates itself." To this purpose the Holy Scripture says, "Truth triumphs over everything."[1]

The moon is a planet which gives influence of melancholy and folly; and because on her account, according to the disposition of the body of men, comes to some the malady of frenzy and melancholy, she is here portrayed pulling against the vale of an arc, and people under her melancholic and frenetic.[2]

10 Phoebe (The Moon)

Text

Never resemble Phoebe;
She is too changeable and hostile
To constancy and strong courage—
Melancholy and lunatic.

Gloss

The moon is called Phoebe, from whom "Monday" is named; and to her is attributed the metal that we call silver. The moon does not stop for any hour in a right degree and gives influence of mutability and folly; and for this wishes to say that the good knight should guard himself against these same vices. And to this purpose says Hermes: "Use wisdom and be constant."

Allegory

Phoebe, who is the moon, that we note for inconstancy, that the good knight ought not to have, and, similarly, the good spirit. As St. Ambrose says in his letter to Simplician, the fool is as changeable as the moon, but the sage is always constant: in a state where he never breaks from fear, he never changes through power; he never raises himself in prosperity; he never plunges himself into sadness. There where is wisdom, there is virtue, strength, and constancy. The wise man is always of one courage; it neither decreases nor increases for change of anything; he does not waver in diverse opinions, but resides faultless in Jesus Christ, founded in charity, enrooted in faith. And to this purpose says Holy Scripture: "A holy man continueth in wisdom as the sun: but a fool is changed as the moon."

---

1 3 Esdras 3:12. In the story of Darius's three bodyguards who argue over which is the strongest--wine, the king, or women--the third adds that truth is victorious over everything.

2 Christine here refers to a manuscript illumination accompanying Fable 10.

Mars is a planet which gives influence of wars and battles, and for this his image is figured here entirely armed and underneath.[1]

11 Mars

Text

Mars, your father, I do not doubt it,
You will follow well in everything;
For your noble condition
Draws from it your inclination.

Gloss

From Mars is the day of *mardi* [Tuesday] named; and to him is attributed the metal which we call iron. Mars is a planet who gives influence of wars and battles. And for this every knight who loves or pursues arms and deeds of chivalry and has renown of valor may be called son of Mars. And for this Othea also names Hector, notwithstanding he was the son of the king Priam, and says that he would well follow his father, that which every good knight ought to do. And a sage declares that through these works of man one may recognize his inclinations.

Allegory

Mars, the god of battle, may well be called the son of God, who victoriously battled in this world. And that the good spirit, through his example, should follow his good father Jesus Christ and battle against vices, declares St. Ambrose in the first book of *The Offices*, that he who would be a friend of God must be an enemy of the devil; he who would have peace with Jesus Christ must have war with the vices. And just as in vain one makes war in the field with foreign enemies there where the city is full of domestic spies, so also may not overcome the evils on the outside who will not battle strongly the sins of his soul; and it is the most glorious victory which may exist when he overcomes his own self. "For your[2] wrestling is not against flesh and blood; but against principalities and powers, against the rulers of the world of this darkness, against the spirits of wickedness in the high places." Ephesians 6[:12]

Mercury is a planet who gives influence of beautiful language; and was called god of language. He holds a flower because just as the flower is naturally pleasing to the sight, so also language well ornamented is pleasing to hear. He has a full purse, for through beautiful language one comes eventually to great riches. So he has under him wise men who speak together. With this ends the seven planets.

---

1 Again, Christine refers to the illumination. Subsequent italicized introductions also so refer and will not be noted.
2 "Our" in the Vulgate/Douay-Rheims.

12 Mercury

Text
Be adorned in eloquence,
And in word clean and pure;
This you will apprehend in Mercury,
Who knows the use of speaking well.

Gloss
From Mercury is named the day of *mercredi* [Wednesday], and quicksilver is attributed to him. Mercury is a planet which gives influence of beautiful language adorned with rhetoric and with pontifical behavior. For this says to the good knight that he ought to be adorned, for honorable behavior and beautiful language much befalls every noble desiring the great prize of honor, as long as he guards himself from speaking too much. For Diogenes says that of all virtues, the more the better, except of speech.

Allegory
Mercury, who is god of language, we may take that the knight Jesus Christ should be adorned with good preaching and with words of doctrine, and also ought to love and honor the announcers thereof. And St. Gregory declares in his *Homilies* that one should hold in great reverence the preachers of Holy Scripture, for they are the couriers who come before our Lord and our Lord follows them. Holy preaching makes the way, and then our Lord comes into the dwelling of our heart; the words of exhortation make the course, and so truth is received into our understanding. And to this purpose our Lord says to his Apostles: "He who heareth you, heareth me, and he that despise you, despiseth me." Luke 10[:16]

13 Minerva

Text
Armors of all kinds
With which to arm, well-made and strong,
By your mother will be delivered to you,
Minerva, who is not bitter[1] to you.

Gloss
Minerva was a lady of very great wisdom and invented the art of armor-making, for previously the people did not arm themselves except with *cuir boulu* [boiled leather]. And for the great knowledge which existed in this lady, they called her goddess.

And because Hector could well put armors to work, and this was his right craft, Othea called him the son of Minerva, notwithstanding he was

---

1 *Amere*, but also not-mother (*a-mere*), which in fact is true of Minerva in relation to Hector; more figuratively, *litotes* or understatement in that mothers are indeed not bitter but instead kind, and arm their sons.

the son to the queen Hecuba of Troy; and through likeness all lovers of arms may be named. And to this purpose says one authority: "Knights given to arms are subjects to them."

Allegory

By this which is stated, that well-made and strong armors will be delivered to the good knight, we may understand the virtue of faith, which is a theological virtue and is mother to the good spirit. And that she delivers enough armors, Cassiodorus says in the *Exposition on the Creed* that faith is the light of the soul, the door of paradise, the window of life, and the foundation of everlasting health, for without faith no one can please God. And to this purpose St. Paul the Apostle speaks: "Without faith it is impossible to please God." Letter to the Hebrews 11[:6]

The goddess Minerva and the goddess Pallas together.

14 Pallas and Minerva

Text

Embrace Pallas the goddess
And reap with your prowess.
All will go well for you if you have her;
Minerva sits well with Pallas.

Gloss

After it says that he joins Pallas with Minerva, who sits well there, and he should know in it that Pallas and Minerva is a similar thing, but the names are taken for two intentions. For the lady who had the name Minerva was also surnamed Pallas from an island that had the name Pallence, from which she was named; and because generally in all things she was wise and invented many new arts, beautiful and subtle, they named her goddess of wisdom. So she is named Minerva in that which appertain to chivalry, and Pallas in all things which appertain to wisdom. And therefore it is said that he should unite wisdom to chivalry, which exists very well according thereto. And as weapons ought to be guarded, may be understood by faith: to this purpose Hermes says: "Join love of faith with wisdom."

Allegory

And just as Pallas, who means wisdom, ought to be joined with chivalry, so also the virtue of hope ought to be joined with the good virtues of the chivalrous spirit, without the which he may not avail. And Origen says in his *Homilies on Exodus* that the hope of the good to come is the solace of those who suffer in this mortal life, just as, for the laborers, hope of payment softens the labor of their tasks, and, for the champions who are in battle, hope of the crown of victory tempers the dolor of their wounds. And to this purpose speaks St. Paul the Apostle: "We may have the strongest comfort, who have fled for refuge to hold fast the hope set before us." Letter to the Hebrews 6[:18]

15 Penthesilea

Text
Have cheer of Penthesilea;
After your death she will be woeful.
Such a woman ought well be a friend,
Of whom so noble a voice is sown.

Gloss
Penthesilea was a maiden, queen of the Amazons, and was very beautiful and of marvelous prowess in arms, and hardy; for the great good which the renown transmitted through all the world of Hector the worthy, this one loved him with very great love, and from the parties of the Orient came to Troy in the time of great siege to see Hector. But when she found him dead, she became despondent out of moderation; and with a very great host of gentlewomen very chivalrously avenged his death, where she performed deeds of marvelous prowess and many great griefs she created for the Greeks. And because she was virtuous, it is said to the good knight that he ought to love her, and this is understood that each good knight ought to love and prize every virtuous person, and similarly a woman strong in virtue of intelligence and constancy. And such a woman is saddened by the death of Hector, which is to understand what prowess and valor is lost in the death of the knight. And a wise man says, "Bounty should be allowed where it is perceived."

Allegory
By Penthesilea, who gave succor, we may understand the virtue of charity, which is the third theological virtue and which the good spirit ought to have perfectly in him. Cassiodorus says that charity is also like the rain which falls in spring, for it distills the drops of the virtues under the which grain good will and good deed fructify. She is patient in adversity, temperate in prosperity, patient in humility, joyous in affliction; she wishes well to her enemies and friends, similarly to her enemies communicating her good. To this purpose speaks St. Paul the Apostle: "Charity is patient, is kind: charity envieth not, dealeth not perversely; is not puffed up; is not ambitious, seeketh not her own." First Letter to the Corinthians 13[:4-5]

Narcissus who beheld himself in the fountain.

16 Narcissus[1]

Text
Do not look to appear as Narcissus

---

1 See also Fable 86, on Echo.

Through putting on too much pride;
For the overly presumptuous knight
Is void of great grace.

Gloss

Narcissus was a bachelor[1] who through his great beauty raised himself
in such great pride that he held in contempt all others. And because he
praised no one but himself, it is said that he was so amorous and besotted
with himself that he died after he beheld himself in the fountain. This is
to understand the excessive presumption in him when he beholds himself.
Through this warns the good knight never to behold himself in his good
deeds, lest he be by it overweeningly proud. And to this purpose says
Socrates: "Son, watch that you do not be deceived in the beauty of your
youth, for it is never an enduring thing."

Allegory

Now let us turn allegory to our purpose, putting to use the seven deadly
sins. Through Narcissus we shall understand the sin of pride, against
which the good spirit ought to guard himself. And Origen declares in his
Homilies: "Why do earth and ashes make him proud, or how dare a man
raise himself up in arrogance, when he thinks from what he is come and
what he will become; and in how frail a vessel is his life contained, and
in what filth is he plunged, and what waste material does he not cease to
throw from his flesh through all the conduits of his body?" And to this
purpose says Holy Scripture: "If his pride mount up even to heaven, and
his head touch the clouds: In the ends he shall be destroyed like a
dunghill." Job [20:6-7]

The king Athamas who through wrath killed his wife and children.

17 Athamas

Text

Athamas, full of great rage—
The goddess of madness—
Tried to strangle these two children;
Against this great ire, defend yourself.

Gloss

Athamas was a king, husband to the queen Ino, who had tried to have
sown roasted seed-corn in order to disinherit her stepchildren, for she had
corrupted with silver the priests of the law who reported the responses of
the gods. So they reported to the king and to those of the country that the
seed that had been sown would never grow; therefore it pleased the gods
that the two beautiful and gentle children that the king had would be driven
away and exiled. And because the king consented to the exile of the two

---

1 *Damoisel*—A bachelor knight who has not yet become a knight.

children, although he did it greatly moved and with a great sorrow, the fable says that the goddess Juno because of it wished to take vengeance and went to the underworld to say to the goddess of madness that she would come to afflict the king Athamas. Then the horrible and frightful goddess came with all her hair full of serpents and set herself on the smoke-hole of the roof of the palace and stretched her arms around the two sides of the door. And then there began such a strife between the king and the queen that they had nearly torn each other apart. And when they thought to run out of the palace, then the maddened goddess drew two horrible serpents from her very foul, coarse hair and threw them in their laps; and when they became wholly afraid of the goddess, then both of the two went mad. Athamas killed the queen in rage and afterwards the two children, and he himself leaped from a high rock into the sea.[1] The exposition of this fable may be that a queen might be so vicious to her stepchildren that she might try to disinherit them through some malice, of which afterwards peace between the father and stepmother may not exist, and perhaps at last he kills them. And because wrath is a deadly vice and so evil that he who is so tainted with it has no understanding of reason, indicates to the good knight that against wrath he must guard himself carefully, for too great a default it is for a good knight to be wrathful. And therefore Aristotle declares: "Keep yourself from wrath, for it troubles the understanding and disturbs reason."

Allegory

By Athamas, who was entirely full of ire, we understand properly the sin of ire, of which the good spirit should be void. And St. Augustine says in a *Letter* that just as vinegar in the barrel corrodes the vessel where it lies if it remains there too long, so also ire corrodes the heart where it enters if it remains there from one day to another. Therefore St. Paul the Apostle says: "Let not the sun go down on your anger." Ephesians 4[:26]

---

1 In Ovid, *Metamorphoses.* 4.420 sq., Athamas marries divine Nephele by order of Juno and produces two children, Phrixus and Helle. However, in love with Ino, he marries her and produces Learchus and Melicertes, and Nephele returns to heaven. Ino plots to get rid of her predecessor's children by roasting the seed-corn which does indeed cause a famine; she bribes the messengers sent to the oracle so that they say Phrixus must be sacrificed. Both Nephele's children escape, but Juno drives Athamas mad, who kills Learchus; and Ino, with Melicertes, leaps into the sea.

Mercury, who transformed Aglauros, his sister-in-law, into stone for her envy.

18 Aglauros

Text

Of everything that you may ever see,[1]
Flee the false goddess envy,
Who made Aglauros, transformed to
Stone, greener than ivy.

Gloss

Aglauros, so says a fable, was a sister to Herse, who was so beautiful that for her beauty she was married to Mercury, the god of language, and they were daughters of Cecrops, the king of Athens. But there was so much envy in Aglauros for her sister Herse, who through her beauty had advanced so far as to be married to the god, that wholly compelled by envy she became dry and discolored and green as a leaf of ivy through the envy which she bore to her sister. One day Aglauros was seated near the threshold of the door and refused entrance to Mercury, who wished to enter into the residence, nor for any prayer that he made to enter would she allow him. Then the god became enraged and said that she might remain there every day, as hard as the heart she had; and then Aglauros became hard as stone. So the fable may be verified through a similar case that happened to several persons. Mercury may be a powerful man, well-spoken, who tries to imprison his sister-in-law or kill her because of some displeasure that she has caused him. And therefore this indicates that she was transformed into stone. And because it is too unsightly a stain and against gentleness to be envious, it says to the good knight that he must guard against it in all things. And Socrates declares: "He who bears the burden of envy has perpetual pain."

Allegory

Just as the authority warns the good spirit against envy, so also Holy Scripture warns the good spirit against the same vice. And St. Augustine states:[2] "Envy is hate of the happiness of another, and the envy of the envious manifests itself against those who are greater than he, because he is not as great as they; against those who are equal to him, because he is not greater than they; and against those who are lesser than he, because of fear that they will wax as great as he." To this purpose Scripture says: "The eye of the envious is wicked; and he turned away his face." Ecclesiasticus 14[:8]

---

1 In Latin, envy, or *invidia*, has as its root *videre*, to see, in that the envious longs to have what he sees another has.

2 *Epistle* 210, *PL* 33: 958.

19 Ulysses and Polyphemus

Text
Do not be long or long-winded;
Beware in yourself the malice
Of Ulysses, who thus stole
The eye of the giant, although he saw clearly.

Gloss
A fable says that when Ulysses was returning to Greece after the destruction of Troy, a great tempest of weather transported the ship to an island where there was a giant who had only one eye in the middle of his forehead, of horrible size. Ulysses through his subtlety stole it and robbed him, that is to understand, punctured it. That is to say that the good knight should guard himself that sloth does not overtake him through the deceits and wiles of the malicious, so that his eye may be by it robbed, that is to understand, the eye of his understanding or his honor, or his goods, or that which he holds dear, as many an inconvenience happens often through sloth and cowardice. And to this purpose Hermes says: "Blessed is he who uses his days in suitable solicitude."

Allegory
Where it is said that the good knight should not be long nor long-winded, we may understand the sin of sloth which the good spirit should not have. For as Bede says in the *Proverbs of Solomon*: "The slothful who does not wish to work for the love of God is not worthy to reign with God, and is not worthy to receive the crown promised to the knights, he who is a coward in undertaking the fields of battle." Therefore Scripture says: "The thoughts of the industrious always bring forth abundance: but every sluggard is always in want." Proverbs 21[:5]

20 Latona

Text
Do not contest with frogs,
Nor soil yourself in their swamp.
Against Latona they assembled,
And they troubled the clear water before her.

Gloss
The fable says that the goddess Latona was the mother of Phoebus and Phoebe, who is the sun and the moon, and she carried them both in her womb. Juno chased her through every country because she was pregnant by Jupiter, her husband. One day the goddess Latona was much harassed, and arrived at a ford; and then she stooped down to the water to quench

her great thirst, where there was gathered a great crowd of serfs[1] bathing in the water from the great heat of the sun, and they tried to insult Latona and troubled the water where she tried to drink, nor had any pity for her predicament. Then she cursed them and said that all their days they might remain in the swamp. Then they were foul and abominable and every day did not cease to bray and scold. Afterwards the serfs became frogs, who may not stop from braying, as it appears in summertime at the riverside. Thus it may be that some peasants caused displeasure to some great mistress, who made them to be thrown in the river and drowned, and so they became frogs. And it is to understand that the good knight should not sully himself in the swamp of villainy, but shun all villainous stains which are contrary to gentleness; for as villainy may not suffer gentleness, accordingly gentleness should not suffer villainy in himself, nor likewise to contend, nor to take debate with a person villainous of conditions, nor to speak outrageously. And Plato says: "He who joins to his gentleness nobility of good conditions is to be praised, and he who allows gentleness which comes from his parents to suffice without acquiring good conditions should not be regarded as noble."

Allegory

The villains who became frogs we may understand as the sin of avarice, which is contrary to the good spirit. For St. Augustine declares that the avaricious man is similar to hell, for hell knows not even so much as to swallow up souls that it says: "That is enough!" And even if all the treasures of the world would be amassed in the possession of the avaricious man, he would not be satisfied. And to this purpose Scripture says: "The eye of the covetous man is insatiable in his portion of iniquity." Ecclesiasticus 14[:9]

21 Bacchus

Text
Never agree with the god Bacchus,
For his terms are foul.
His pleasures are not worthwhile;
He makes people transform into swine.

Gloss
Bacchus was a man who first planted vines in Greece; and when they of the country felt the strength of the wine which made them drunk, they said that Bacchus was a god, who had given such strength to his plant. Thus by Bacchus is understood drunkenness, as this is a very impertinent

---

1 *Villains*, which Christine intends to mean "serfs" who are not gentlemen and also "wretches," villains in the modern sense.

thing and great vice to every noble man who would use reason. And to this purpose Ypocras[1] says: "Excessive wine and viands destroy the body, the soul, and the virtues."

Allegory

Through the god Bacchus we may note the sin of gluttony, from which the good spirit should keep himself. "Gluttony," declares St. Gregory in his *Morals*, "and when the vice of gluttony seizes the mastery of a person, he loses all the good that he has done; and when the belly is not restrained by abstinence, all the virtues are drowned." Therefore St. Paul says: "Whose end is destruction; whose God is their belly; and whose glory is in their shame; who mind earthly things." To the Philippians [3:19]

22 Pygmalion

Text

Do not be besotted with the image
Of Pygmalion, if you are wise,
For the equal of such an image
Is beauty beyond compare.

Gloss

Pygmalion was a very subtle worker of fair images; and a fable says that, from the great vileness which he saw in the women of Sidon, he despised them and declared that he would create an image of a woman of sovereign beauty. When he had perfected it, Love, who knows how to ravish hearts subtly, caused him to be enamored with his image, so that for her he was afflicted with the maladies of love, full of complaints and piteous sighings that he made to her; but the image, which was of stone, did not understand him. To the temple of Venus Pygmalion went, and made there such a devout complaint that the goddess had pity; and, in demonstration of this, the brand that she held by herself caught fire and burned. Then because of the sign the lover was joyous, and toward his image he went, and took her in his arms, and warmed her with his naked flesh so entirely that the image had life, and began to speak. And so Pygmalion had recovered joy. To this fable may be set many expositions, and similarly to other such fables. And because the poets made them so that the understanding of men would be sharpened and made subtle to find there diverse expositions, so it may be understood that Pygmalion despised the vileness of unchaste women and became enamored of a maiden of very great beauty, one who did not wish or could not understand his piteous complaints, not that she was of stone. The image had been created; that is, through thinking of these exquisite beauties he became enamored. At the last, he prayed to her so much and kept him so near her

---

1 Hippocrates was usually called "Ypocras," also the name of a medicinal postprandial liqueur.

that the maiden loved him at his will and had him in marriage. Thus the image that was hard as stone recovered life through the goddess Venus. So it would say that the good knight ought not to be besotted with such a created image in such a manner that he abandons following the crafts of arms, to which he is obliged by the order of chivalry. And to this purpose Apthalin says: "An impertinent situation it is when a prince is besotted with a thing which makes him reprehensible."

Allegory
Pygmalion's image, with which the good knight should not besot himself, we take as the sin of lechery, against which the chivalrous spirit ought to guard his body. About lechery St. Jerome said in a *Letter*: "O fire of hell, of which the wood is gluttony; the flame is pride; the sparks are corrupt words; the smoke is evil reputation; the cinders are poverty; and the end is the torment of hell." To this purpose declares St. Peter the Apostle: "... counting for a pleasure the delights of a day: stains with spots, sporting themselves to excess, rioting in their feasts with you." 2 Peter 2[:13]

23 Diana (The Moon)

Text
Of Diana be mindful,
For honesty of your body,[1]
For a soiled life does not please her,
Nor one dishonest or unclean.

Gloss
Diana, that is, the moon, and as there exists nothing so evil that it does not have some good property, the moon gives chaste conditions; and they named it after a lady called so, who was very chaste and virgin all her days. So this wishes to say that honesty of body belongs well to the good knight. To this purpose says Hermes: "He may not be of perfect sense who in himself will not have chastity."

Allegory
And to recall to the allegory the articles of faith to our purpose, without the which the good spirit may not profit, we shall take for Diana God of paradise, the which is without any spot of unclean love, to whom a thing soiled from sin may not be agreeable, creator of heaven and of earth, the which thing is necessary to the chivalrous spirit. So says the first Article of Faith, which my lord St. Peter declares: "I believe in God the Father omnipotent, creator of heaven and earth."

---

1 *Cors*, body, both rhymes and plays with mindful, *recors*—"re-body yourself" in chastity.

24 Ceres

Text
Resemble the goddess Ceres,
Who gives them corn, but not sown by anyone;
The good knight well-ordered[1]
Also ought to be generous.

Gloss
Ceres was a lady who invented the art of tilling the land, for before, they sowed the arable lands without a plough. And because the earth bore more abundantly after it had been tilled, they declared that she was the goddess of corn, and they named the earth after her name. So this wishes to say, just as earth is abundant and a large donor of all goods, so also the good knight should be liberal to all persons and give his aid and comfort according to his ability. And Aristotle says: "Be a generous giver and you will have friends."

Allegory
We shall take for Ceres, whom the good knight should resemble, the blessed Son of God whom the good spirit ought to follow, who has given so liberally to all of us of his high goods, and in him should be believed firmly. So says the second Article which St. John tells, where he says: "And in Jesus Christ, his only begotten son, our Lord."

25 Isis

Text
All high virtues set and plant
In you, as Isis made the plants
And all the grains fructify;
So also you should edify.

Gloss
Isis, so also the poets say, that she is goddess of plants and of cultivating, and gives them strength and increase to multiply. For this says to the good knight that also he ought to fructify in all virtues and avoid evil vice. And Hermes says to this purpose: "O man, if you knew the inconvenience of vice, how you would guard against it; and if you understand the reward for valor, how you would love it."

Allegory
There where it says that the good spirit ought to resemble Isis, who is a planter, we may understand the holy conception of Jesus Christ by the Holy Spirit in the holy Virgin Mary, mother of all grace, from whom the great bounties may not be imagined and said wholly; the which worthy

---

1 *Ordonnez*, ordered, ordained, which plays with *donne*, gives, and *abandonnez*, abundant, to compare the giving of Ceres with the spiritual, ordered giving of the soul.

Conception the good spirit ought to have wholly in himself, and hold firmly the worthy Article, as says St. James the Greater: "Who is conceived by the Holy Ghost, is born of the Virgin Mary."

26 Midas

Text

Do not hold to the judgment
Of Midas, who never judged
Wisely; so do not counsel yourself by it,
For he earned by it the ears of an ass.

Gloss

Midas was a king who had little understanding, and a fable declares that Phoebus and Pan, the god of shepherds, competed together, and Phoebus said that the sound of the lyre deserved greater praise than the sound of the flute or pipe. Pan supported the opposite and said that the flute deserved greater praise. They looked upon Midas in this discord and they made him judge; and after both of them had played before Midas, at long last he judged that the sound of the flute was more worthy and pleased more than that of the harp. Thus the fable says that Phoebus, who was angered, expressed contempt for his rude understanding, and fashioned him ears of an ass in demonstration of his asinine understanding that had judged so foolishly. And it may be that each judges foolishly against a prince or powerful man, the which punished him by making him to bear on him some sign of a fool, which is understood by the ears of an ass. Also it is to understand by this fable that the good knight should not hold to a foolish judgment not founded on reason, nor likewise should he be the judge of so faulty a sentence. To this purpose a philosopher states: "The fool is like a mole which hears and does not understand." And Diogenes compares the fool to a stone.

Allegory

By the judgment of Midas, which the good knight should not hold, we may understand Pilate, who judged the blessed Son of God to be strung like a lyre and hung on the gibbet of the Cross like a thief,[1] he who was pure without stain. Also it is to understand that the good spirit watches how he judges the innocent; and should believe the Article that St. Andrew declares: "He passed before Pontius Pilate, was crucified, died, and buried."

27 Pirothous and Theseus

Text

If you have loyal companions in arms,
Down into hell where men of arms go,

---

1 Thief, "lierres," hung on the cross in counter to Christ the *lier*, or lyre, Word of God.

You ought to go, to aid them
In need, as did Hercules.

Gloss

The fable says that Pirothous and Theseus descended into hell to rescue Proserpina whom Pluto had ravished; and they would have been mistreated there if Hercules, who had been their companion in the past, had not aided them, who so wholly performed there feats of arms that he frightened all the infernal inhabitants, and had Cerberus the doorkeeper cut the chains. So it is said that the good knight ought not to fail his loyal companion for doubt of whichever peril that might be, for loyal companions should be as one and the same thing. And says Pythagoras: "You ought to guard love of your friend diligently."

Allegory

By the authority which says that he ought to aid the loyal companions of arms into hell, we may understand the blessed soul of Jesus Christ, who took away the good souls of the holy patriarchs and fathers who were in limbo there. And by example ought the good spirit draw to him all virtues and believe the Article that St. Philip declares: "He descended into hell."

28 Cadmus

Text

Cadmus was very loved and prized,
And, so his teaching may be authorized,
Let them exist in you, for he won
The fountain from the serpent with great difficulty.

Gloss

Cadmus was a very noble man and founded Thebes, which was a city of great renown. He established a school there, and in him, similarly, there existed much of letters and of great knowledge; and for this the fable says that he mastered the serpent at the fountain. This is to understand knowledge and wisdom which always flows up; the serpent is noted for the pain and travail that he assembles for the student also to master who has acquired knowledge. And the fable says that he similarly divined the serpent, which is to understand that he was master and corrector of others. So Othea wishes to say that the good knight ought to love and honor the letters of the clerks, which are founded on sciences. To this purpose Aristotle said to Alexander: "Honor wisdom and fortify it through good masters."

Allegory

By Cadmus, who mastered the serpent at the fountain, which the good knight ought to love, we may understand the blessed humanity of Jesus Christ, who mastered the serpent and won the fountain, that is, the life of the world, which he passed in great difficulty and in great travail, for which he had perfect victory, when he was resurrected on the third day, so that St. Thomas says, "On the third day he rose from the dead."

29 Io

Text

Delight yourself greatly in the knowledge of
Io, who has more than any other,
For through it you may apprehend much
And of the good in it take largely.

Gloss

Io was a gentlewoman, daughter of King Inachus, who inherited greatly of extensive knowledge and invented many manners of letters of the alphabet which had not been seen before. How that several fables say that Io was a woman friend of Jupiter and that she became a cow and afterwards became a common woman. But as the poets have hidden truth under cover of fable, it can be understood that Jupiter loved her, that is to mean, the virtues of Jupiter which existed in her. She became a cow, for just as the cow gives milk, which is sweet and nourishing, she gave, through the letters which she invented, sweet nourishment to the understanding. That she became a common woman can be understood in that her sense was common to all, as letters are common to all people. For this means that the good knight ought to esteem Io greatly, who can be understood as letters and writings and histories of good folk which the good knight ought to hear told willingly, the example of which may be valuable to him. And to this purpose Hermes says, "Whoever forces himself to acquire knowledge and good conditions, he will find that which pleases him in the world and in the other [world]."

Allegory

Io, who is understood through letters and writing, we may understand as the good spirit who should delight in reading or hearing the Holy Scriptures and should have written down his thought, and through this may apprehend how to ascend to heaven with Jesus Christ through good works and holy contemplation. And [the good spirit] should believe the worthy Article which St. Bartholomew states: "He ascended up to heaven, he sat at the right hand of God the Father omnipotent."

30 Mercury and Argus

Text

Watch in whatever place that you may be,
That you do not become sleepy from the sound of flutes;

Mercury, who sings softly,
Enchants people with his flute.

Gloss

A fable relays that when Jupiter loved Io the beautiful, Juno had very great suspicion of him, and descended from heaven in a cloud to surprise her husband with the deed. But when Jupiter saw her coming, he changed his beloved into a cow; but for all that the change was not out of her thought, and she asked that he give the cow to her. And Jupiter contrary to his heart granted it to her, as he did not want to refuse her for doubt of suspicion. Then Juno gave her cow to Argus, her cowherd who had a hundred eyes, to guard, and always he watched her. But the god Mercury, by the commandment of Jupiter, took his flute, which sang softly, and blew so long into the ear of Argus that all of his hundred eyes, one after the other, fell asleep; afterwards, he took away the cow and cut off his [Argus's] head. The exposition of this fable may be that some strong man loved a gentlewoman so that his wife took up guarding him that her husband might not be deceived, and set great guards and clear seers, who may be understood as the eyes of Argus. But the beloved, through a malicious and well-speaking person, did so much that the guards consented to give him his love, and afterwards they fell asleep from the fluting of Mercury and had their heads cut off. Therefore it is said to the good knight that he should not fall asleep from such a flute so that he is robbed of that which he should well guard. And to this purpose says Hermes: "Keep away from those who govern themselves by malice."

Allegory

By the fluting of Mercury we may understand that the good spirit is not deceived through the ancient enemy by any incredulity in faith or otherwise. And he should believe firmly the Article that St. Matthew the Evangelist says, who says that God will come to judge the living and the dead, where he declares, "Whence he will come to judge the living and the dead."

31 Pyrrhus

Text

Believe that Pyrrhus will resemble
His father, and again he will trouble
His enemies by aggrieving them;
He will avenge the death of Achilles.

Gloss

Pyrrhus was a son of Achilles and keenly resembled his father in strength and hardiness; and after the death of his father he went to Troy and very harshly avenged his father and greatly injured the Trojans. Therefore this [fable] would say to the good knight that, if he has acted badly toward his father, he should beware of the son when he comes of age. And if the father has been valiant, the son should be the same. To this purpose declares a sage: "The death of the father attracts the vengeance of the son."

Allegory

There where he says that Pyrrhus will resemble his father, we may understand the Holy Spirit, which proceeds from the Father, in which the good spirit ought to believe firmly, as says St. James the Lesser: "I believe in the Holy Ghost."

32 Cassandra

Text

Frequent the temple and honor
The gods of heaven at all hours,
And uphold the practice of Cassandra,
If you would be held wise.

Gloss

Cassandra was a daughter to the king Priam,[1] and she was a very good lady and devout in their law. She served the gods and honored the temple, and spoke little without cause. And when she felt it appropriate to speak, she only said things which were true; she was never found lying. Cassandra was full of great knowledge, therefore it indicates to the good knight that he should resemble her, for foolish customs and lying words create much to blame in a knight. So he ought to serve God and honor the temple, that is, to understand the Church and its ministers. And Pythagoras says: "A most praiseworthy thing it is to serve God and sanctify the saints."

Allegory

The authority says that the good knight should frequent the temple; similarly, the good spirit ought to do, and ought to have singular devotion in the holy catholic Church and in the communion of the saints. As the Article declares which St. Symon says, which is: "One holy catholic church, a communion of saints."

33 Neptune

Text

If you often frequent the sea,
You ought to invoke Neptune;
And celebrate well his festival,
So that he may protect you from storm.

---

1 And therefore sister to Hector.

Gloss

Neptune, in accord with the law of the pagans, was called the god of the sea, and therefore it is said to the good knight that he ought to serve him, that is to understand that the knights who frequently travel on many voyages to the sea or in other diverse perils have greater necessity to be devout and to serve God and the saints than other people, to the extent that in their need he may be helpful and in aid to them. And they should take a singular devotion to some saint by devout prayers, through which they may petition him in their need. And that the prayer of the heart may not alone suffice, the wise man says: "I never deem God to be well served only by words, but by good deeds."

Allegory

Neptune, whom the good knight should invoke if he travels often on the sea, we shall take as the good spirit continually on the sea of the world, who ought to devoutly petition his creator and pray that if he should live that he may have remission of his sins. And he should believe the Article that St. Jude declares: "The remission of sins."

34 Atropos

Text

Have regard at every hour
For Atropos and for his[1] sting,
Who is savage and spares not even a soul—
Who will make you think about the soul.

Gloss

The poets name death "Atropos;" therefore this would say to the good knight that he should think that every day he shall never live in this world, but will soon depart from it. So he ought to have greater concern for the virtues of the soul than to delight himself in the pleasures of the body; and every Christian should think of this, to the extent that he has in memory the provision of the soul, which will endure without end. And to this purpose Pythagoras says that, just as our beginning comes from God, it is appropriate that our end will be there.

Allegory

There where it is said to the good knight that he should have regard for Atropos, who is noted as death, the good spirit should have the same, who through the merits of the Passion of our Lord Jesus Christ should hold steadfast hope, with the pain and diligence that he should set to have paradise at the end. And he ought to believe firmly that he will be

---

1 Christine changes the gender of Atropos, one of the three traditionally female spinning Fates, to male. Atropos is the last of three sisters—Clotho, who spins out a life, Lachesis, who measures it out, and Atropos, who snips it short.

resurrected on the day of judgment and will have life enduring, if he deserve it. As St. Matthew states in the final Article, "The resurrection of the flesh, eternal life. Amen."

35 Bellerophon

Text

Bellerophon is exemplary
In all the deeds that you would like to perform,
Who prefers to desire to die
Than to encourage disloyalty.

Gloss

Bellerophon was a knight of very great beauty and full of loyalty. His stepmother[1] was so seized by love for him that she required it of him and, because he would not consent to her will, she did so much that he was condemned to be devoured by fierce beasts; and he preferred to choose death than to express disloyalty. To this purpose Hermes declares: "Better you wish to mourn without cause than to perform an unfitting deed."

Allegory

Now we come to declare the Commandments of the law, and by it we shall take allegory to our purpose.

Bellerophon, who was so full of loyalty, may signify God in paradise; and, as his worthy mercy has been to us and is full of all loyalty, we may by it take the First Commandment, which says, "You shall worship no strange gods." That is to say, as St. Augustine declares: "The honor which is named 'devotion of heart' you should not bear either to an idol or an image or a likeness of to any creature; for that is an honor due only to God, and in this commandment all idolatry is forbidden."[2] About this our Lord says in the Gospel: "The Lord thy God shalt thou adore, and him only shalt thou serve." Matthew 4[:10]

36 Memnon[3]

Text

Memnon, your loyal cousin,
Who in your need is neighbor to you
And loves you so much, you should respect
And for his need arm yourself.

---

1 Christine, using as her source the *Ovide moralisé* 4. 5941-6, according to Loukopoulos, confuses Bellerophon with Hippolytus (loved by his stepmother Phaedra) because of the biblical model of Potiphar's wife.

2 *The City of God* 6, Preface; "devotion of the heart" is the way Babyngton translates *latrie*, which is untranslatable, but which has the force of "decree."

3 The son of Aurora. See Fable 44.

Gloss

The king Memnon was cousin to Hector, of the Trojan line, and when Hector engaged in fierce battles, where he was many a time harshly oppressed by his enemies, Memnon, who was a very valiant knight, followed close to him; so much he aided Hector and crushed the great presses. And in this he performed well, for when Achilles had killed him in treason, Memnon wounded Achilles harshly and would have slain him if brief succor had not come to him. Therefore it is said to the good knight that he ought to respect him and succor him in his need; and it is to understand that every prince and every knight who has a relative, however small or poor that he may be, if good and loyal, he ought to respect him and support him in his affairs, and especially when he senses him to be true to him. And it happens sometimes that a great prince is better loved, and more loyally, by his poor relative than by a very powerful man. And to this purpose declares the philosopher Rabion: "Multiply friends, for they will aid you."

Allegory

By Memnon, the loyal cousin, we may understand God in paradise, who has been for us a fully loyal cousin to assume our humanity, the which benefit we may not repay. Thus here we may take the Second Commandment, which says: "Thou shalt not take the name of God in vain." That is to say, as says St. Augustine, "You will never swear dishonestly, or without cause, or for color of falsity, for there may not be a greater wicked practice than to bring to the testimony of a false one the sovereign and very steadfast truth." And in this Commandment is prohibited all lying, all perjury, all blasphemy. To this purpose the law declares: "Thou shalt not take the name of the Lord they God in vain." Exodus 20[:7]

37 Laomedon[1]

Text
Think thus about words
Of great menace, stupid and foul,
Which issue from your mouth in saying too much,
And consider Laomedon.

Gloss

Laomedon was [king] of Troy and father to Priam. And when Jason and his companions journeyed to Colchos to seek the golden fleece and they had arrived and descended to the port of Troy to refresh them without doing any harm to the country, then Laomedon, not well advised, sent messages injuriously dismissing and strongly menacing, if they would not leave in haste from the country. Then the Greek barons because of this

---

1 See also Fable 61.

dismissal took themselves to be so injured that after that followed the destruction of the first Troy. Therefore it is said to the good knight that, as the word of threat may be offensive and villainous, it ought to be carefully weighed before it is spoken, for many a great injury frequently follows thereafter. To this purpose says the poet Hermes: "He is wise who knows how to bridle his mouth."

Allegory

As a word of great menace comes from arrogance, and to break the Commandment is also overweening pride, we may understand that no one should break the feast-day, for it is against the commandment that says: "Remember that you keep holy the day of the sabbath." "Because we are commanded," states St. Augustine, "to keep holy Sunday instead of the sabbath of the Jews, we ought to keep it solemn in repose of the body and in cessation of all our servile works, and in repose of the soul, in cessation of all sins." And about this repose Isaiah the prophet speaks: "Cease to do perversely,
Learn to do well." [Isaiah 1:16-17]

38 Pyramus and Thisbe

Text

Trust nothing to be certain
Until the truth is reached;
For a little presumption
Pyramus makes mention of it to you.

Gloss

Pyramus was a young gentleman of the city of Babylon, and ever since he had been seven years of age, Love had wounded him with his dart and he was taken with love of Thisbe, a beautiful and gentle maiden, and his equal in age and kin. And because of the great frequency of the two lovers together, their great love was perceived and accused by a servant to the mother of the gentle maiden, who took her daughter and closed her up in her room and told her to watch well against the visiting of Pyramus. There was great sadness of the two young people for this reason, and their complaints and laments very piteous. For a long time this prison lasted, but as their age increased, the amorous inclination caught fire from a spark in them, which, despite their long separation, had never been extinguished. But as between the palaces of the parents of the two lovers there was only a thin wall, Thisbe observed the wall perforated so that one saw the light on the other side. There she took the pendant of her belt through the crevice to the extent that her friend might perceive it, as he did shortly enough, and there the two lovers often assembled for very piteous complaints. At the last, because too constrained by their love, their accord was that at night, in the first quarter, they would leave their parents and gather under a white mulberry outside the city at a fountain where in their childhood they used to play. When Thisbe was come to the fountain, alone and fearful, and she heard a lion coming very violently, then she, full of fear, flew away to hide in a bush nearby; but on the way her white wimple[1] fell from her. Pyramus came, who by the light of the moon perceived the wimple, but it had been all dirtied and bloodied by the lion, who had on it vomited the entrails of a beast which he had devoured. Beyond measure the dolor of Pyramus was great, who believed his beloved had been devoured by a fierce beast; thus, after many piteous complaints, he killed himself with his sword. Thisbe sallied forth from the bush, but when she perceived the blood of her lover who was dying, and she saw the sword and the blood, then with great sadness she fell on top of her lover, who could not speak to her. And after many great complaints, regrets, and sighs, killed herself with the same sword. And the fable says that out of pity for her the mulberry then became dark, which used to be white. And because through small occasion happened such a great evil adventure, it says to the good knight that he should not give great faith to a small sign. To this purpose says a sage: "Never yield to some things which are in doubt before you have obtained appropriate information."

Allegory

There where he says that he does not believe to be certain, we may understand the ignorance wherein we are under the correction of father and mother. And for the good deeds that we receive from them, we ought to understand the Fourth Commandment, which says: "Honour thy father and thy mother." That St. Augustine expounds in saying that we ought to honor our parents in two manners, in bearing to them due reverence and in administering to their needs. To this purpose declares the wise man: "Honour thy father and thy mother, that thou mayest be long-lived." [Exodus 20:12]

39 Aesculapius and Circe

Text
Believe, for the health of your body,
The reports of Aesculapius,
And not in the enchantress
Circe, who is too much a deceiver.

Gloss
Aesculapius was a very wise clerk, who discovered the art of medicine and about it made books. And therefore it says to the good knight that he believe the reports on his health; that is to understand, if he have need, that he turn to the doctors and physicians and never to the sorceress Circe, who was a female enchanter. And it may be said for them who in their maladies use sorceries, charms, and enchantments, and believe through

---

1 Head covering or veil fashionable at the time.

them to have protection, which is a thing prohibited and against the Commandments of the Holy Church, and that no good Christian should use. Plato repudiated and burned the books of enchantment and of sorcery made about medicine which at one time had been used, and approved and held himself to those of reasonable science and of experience.

Allegory
Through Aesculapius, who was a physician and surgeon, we may understand the Fifth Commandment, which says, "Thou shalt not kill." And that is to say, so says St. Augustine, neither in heart nor by tongue, nor by hand. And so is prohibited all violent persecution and bodily injuries. And it is not so prohibited to princes, judges, and masters of justice to send to death evil-doers, but entirely alone to them who have thereof no authority, except in case of necessity, wherein a man may not thereof otherwise escape, in which case the right suffer well the defender of himself to kill the other in his body, otherwise not. To this purpose says the Gospel: "He that shall kill by the sword, must be killed by the sword." [Apocalypse 13:10]

40 The Death of Achilles

Text
Him against whom you have done too much,
Who may not thereof avenge it,
Do not trust, for evil from it may fall.
The death of Achilles informs you of it.

Gloss
Achilles gave very great griefs to the Trojans and killed many of the children of King Priam, Hector, Troilus, and the others, for which he deserved hate. Notwithstanding this, Achilles trusted in the queen Hecuba, wife of Priam, whose children he had killed in treason, and went in the night to speak to her about contracting marriage between Polyxena, her daughter, and himself. And there Achilles was killed by Paris and his companions by commandment of the queen, his mother, in the temple of Apollo. For this says to the good knight he should not trust in his enemy who has done against him too much, without making to him peace, or amends. To this purpose says a sage: "Guard yourself against the watches of your enemy who may not avenge himself."

Allegory
As in that one to whom he has done so much that he should not trust him, we shall take that, when we may doubt the vengeance of God, it is necessary to keep the Commandment that says: "You shall do no misconduct," that is to say, of adultery or fornication. And through this is prohibited, as Isidore declares, all illicit carnal coupling, which is outside marriage, and all excessive usage of genitary members. To this purpose

says the law: "Let them be put to death, both the adulterer and the adulteress." Leviticus 20[:10]

41 Busiris

Text

Never resemble Busiris,
Who did greater evil than a thief;
His cruelty invites criticism.
By such deeds do not wish to be caught.

Gloss

Busiris was a king of marvelous cruelty and greatly he delighted in killing men; and indeed he himself in his temples killed them with knives and by this means made a sacrifice to his gods. For this says to the good knight that nothing ought to delight him in killing of human nature, for such cruelty is against God, against nature, and against all goodness. To this purpose Socrates says to the good counselor: "If your prince is cruel, you ought to moderate him through good examples."

Allegory

Busiris, who committed homicides and contrary to human nature, we may understand and note the prohibition that we follow the commandment which says: "Thou shalt not steal." And in this is prohibited, so says St. Augustine, all illicit usurpation of the things of another, all sacrilege, all rapine, all things taken away by force and by mastery over the people without reason. And to this purpose says St. Paul the Apostle: "He that stole, let him now steal no more." Ephesians 4[:28]

42 Leander and Hero

Text

Do not hold so dear your delight
That you set in too great a balance
Your life, which you should love;
Leander perished in the sea.

Gloss

Leander was a young gentleman who loved too much with a great passion Hero the beautiful; and as there was an arm of the sea between the manors of the two lovers, Leander passed it swimming all the night very many a time to see his lady, who had her castle close by the river, so that their love should not be perceived. But it happened that a great weather storm arose, which for several days endured in the sea, that interrupted the joy of the two lovers. And it happened one night that Leander, constrained by too great a desire, took to the sea during the weather storm, and was carried so long there by the perilous waves that he perished piteously. Hero, who was on the other side in great concern for her love, when she saw the body come floating on the river then became distressed by such a marvelous sadness that she threw herself into the sea, and in embracing the perished body drowned. Therefore it is said to the good knight that he should not revere his pleasure to the extent that through it he set his life at too great a risk. So says a sage: "I marvel that I see so many perils suffered for the pleasure of the body, and so little purveyance made for the soul, which is eternal."

Allegory

As the authority prohibits that he hold so dear his pleasure, may be understood the Commandment that says: "Thou shalt not bear false witness against thy neighbour." And so is prohibited, as St. Augustine says, all false accusation, murmuring, detraction, all false reports and defamation of another. And it is to say, as Isidore declares, that the false witness causes villainy to three parties, that is to say, to God, whom he despises in his perjuring; to the judge, whom he deceives in lying; and to his neighbor, whom he hurts in falsely deposing against him. Therefore says Scripture: "A false witness shall not be unpunished: and he that speaketh lies shall not escape." Proverbs 19[:5]

43 Helen

Text

Give up Helen if someone asks for her,
For in a great misdeed lies amends,
And better it is to consent to peace
Than to encourage disloyalty.[1]

Gloss

Helen was wife to the king Menelaus and ravished by Paris in Greece. And when the Greeks were come upon Troy in a great army in vengeance for that deed, before they did any misdeed to the land, they required that Helen be rendered to them and amends made to them for this offense, or else they would destroy the country. And because the Trojans would not do it ensued the great mischief which afterwards came to them. For this wishes to say to the good knight that, if he has begun in folly, it is better for him to leave it and to make peace than to pursue it, so that evil will not befall him as a result. For this Plato the philosopher says: "If you have done wrong to whomever that may be, you should not be at ease until you make accord with him and make peace."

Allegory

By Helen, who should be rendered, may be understood the Commandment which states: "Neither shalt thou desire thy neighbour's wife." For the which is prohibited, as St. Augustine says, the thought and the will to commit fornication, of which the deed is prohibited according to the Sixth

---

1 Alternatively (as written in the right margin), "Than to come to repent too late."

Commandment. For our Lord declares in the Gospel: "Whosoever shall look on a woman to lust after her, hath already committed adultery with her in his heart." Matthew 5[:28]

44 Aurora

Text

Do not resemble the goddess
Aurora, who gives great joy
To others when her hour comes,
But within herself holds sadness and weeping.

Gloss

Aurora, that is the [first] moment of the day; and the fables say that she is a goddess and that she had one of her own sons killed in the battle of Troy, who was named Cygnus; and she, who had power like a goddess, transformed the body of her son into a swan, and from that come the first swans.[1] This lady was of such great beauty that she gladdened all those who saw her, but all her life she mourned her son Cygnus. For this says that the good knight who through his good virtues gladdens others ought not to be sad but joyous and gracefully joyful. For this Aristotle says to Alexander the Great: "Whatever sadness that your heart holds, you should show a joyful face every day to your people."

Allegory

By Aurora who weeps we may understand that no desire for coveting a worldly thing should weep in us. And by this we may note the Tenth Commandment, which says: "Thou shalt not covet thy neighbour's house, nor his ox, nor his ass, not anything that is his." By which, as St. Augustine says, is prohibited the intent to commit theft or rapine, which deed has been prohibited before by the Seventh Commandment. To his purpose says David in his Psalter: "Trust not in iniquity, and cover not robberies." [Psalm 61:11]

45 Pasiphae

Text

For all that Pasiphae was a fool,
Do not try to read in your school
That all women may be like her,
For there exists many a valiant lady.

Gloss

Pasiphae was a queen; and some fables say that she was a woman of great dissolution, and especially that she loved a bull, which is to under-

---

1 Aurora's son was in fact Memnon (Fable 36); Cygnus was, however, changed into a swan after his death in the Trojan war. Both stories appear in Book Twelve of the *Ovide moralisé*.

stand that she had relations with a man of vile condition, by whom she conceived a son of great cruelty and marvelous force. And because he had form of a man and nature of a bull, in that he was strong and of great sharpness and so evil that all the country exiled him, the poets say by fiction that he was half man, half bull. And therefore, though that lady was of such condition, it is said to the good knight that he should not say or sustain that all women are like her, as the truth is manifested to the contrary. Galen learned the science of medicine from a very valiant and wise woman named Cleopatra, who taught him to distinguish many good herbs and their properties.

Allegory
Pasiphae, who was a fool, we may take as the soul returned to God. And St. Gregory says in his *Homilies* that in heaven they have greater joy for a soul returned to God than for a just man who all his days before has been [just]; as the captain in the battle loves more the knight who has fled and afterwards returned, and after his return has severely wounded the enemy, than him who has never performed any beautiful deed; and just as the laborer loves better the earth that, after thorns, bears fruit abundantly, than that which has never had thorns and has never borne fruit. To this purpose God says through the prophet: "They may return every man from his wicked way: and I will forgive their iniquity, and their sin." Jeremiah [36:3]

46 Adrastus

Text
If you have daughters to marry,
And you need to ally them
With men, so that harm will not come to you,
Recall the king Adrastus.

Gloss
Adrastus was a king of Argos, and very powerful and wise. Two knights, one named Polynices and the other Tydeus, fought in the dark night under the gate of his palace; and the one disputed in arms the camp of the other because of violent weather and a great rain which had tormented them all night, and there they had set up for adventure at that hour. The king got up from his bed, when he heard the noise of the swords on the shields, came to disperse the two knights, and between them made good peace. Polynices was son of the king of Thebes and Tydeus of another king of Greece, but they were exiled from their countries. The two barons greatly honored Adrastus and afterwards he gave to them in marriage the two very beautiful daughters which he had. Thereafter, in order to set Polynices in the right of his country which Eteocles his brother held, the king Adrastus made a great army and journeyed to Thebes with a great host. But so much harm ensued of that that all of that host was

greatly discomfited, and dead and taken were all of them, and the two sons-in-law of the king dead. And the brothers, between whom the discord existed, slew the other in battle, and of all the force of Adrastus only remained three of the knights with him. And because there is much to do to set again in their right an exiled people, it is said to the good knight that in such a situation he should have counsel and he should behold himself in this related adventure. And how Adrastus dreamed one night that he gave two daughters in marriage to a lion and a dragon, who fight together, says the expositor of dreams that a dream comes from fantasy in the brain, which may be manifestation of good or evil adventure that is to befall creatures.

Allegory

Where it is said that the daughters have to marry, so that he watches to whom he will give them, we may understand that the good knight of God should well examine with whom he associates, if it happens that in fellowship he would go as did the good Tobias; also every man ought to fix his thoughts on God and on the meditations of the saints. And St. Augustine in a Letter declares that those who have learned from our Lord to be debonaire and humble profit more in meditating and in praying than he does only in reading and hearing. Therefore David says in his Psalter: "I meditated also in thy commandments, which I loved." [Psalms 118:43]

47 Cupid

Text

With Cupid, who is young and
Gallant, it pleases me enough that you acquaint yourself.
How he acts with measure
Pleases well the god of battle.

Gloss

Cupid, that is, the god of love, and because it never sits ill that a young knight is amorous with a lady honored and wise, for his conditions may become much the better when he pulls back to keep the middle way, and which is a thing agreeable enough in arms, it is said to the good knight that she consent sufficiently so that he acquaint himself with Cupid. And a philosopher states that love with good courage comes from a noble heart.

Allegory

That which pleases well the god of battle so that he acquaints himself with Cupid may be understood as penitence. If the good spirit, repentant of his sins, battles against the vices, is young and newly-entered on the right way, he pleases well the god of battle, that is, Jesus Christ, so that he acquaints himself with penitence, and so that Jesus Christ, through his worthy battle, becomes our redeemer. St. Bernard declares: "What word," says he, "of greater mercy may one say to the sinner, who was damned, so that there where he has been sold through sin to the Adversary of hell and may not have any way to redeem himself, than that which God the Father says to him: 'Take my Son and let him battle for you'; and the Son says to him: 'Take me and redeem yourself through me.'" And St. Peter the Apostle recalls this in his first Letter: "Knowing that you were not redeemed with corruptible things as gold or silver....

But with the precious Word of Christ, as of a lamb unspotted and undefiled." St. Peter 1[:18-19]

48 Coronis

Text
Do not kill Coronis the beautiful
Because of the report and the news
Of the crow, for if you kill her,
Afterwards you will repent it.

Gloss
Coronis was a gentlewoman, as a fable declares, who loved Phoebus as a paramour. The crow, who then served him, reported to him that he had seen the beautiful Coronis, his love, sleep with another young man. Because of this news Phoebus became so very sad that he killed his love as soon as she came before him. But afterwards he repented wonderfully, during which the crow, who intended to have reward from his lord for this good deed, was cursed and driven away, and his feathers, which had been usually white as snow, Phoebus changed to black, as sign of sadness; and thus ordained him thereafter to be a bearer and announcer of bad news. And the exposition may be understood so that the servant of some powerful man reported to him similar news, because of which he was driven away and undone. Therefore it is said to the good knight that he should not advance himself by telling to his prince news which might move him to wrath or anger through flattery against the good of another, for in the end, in such reports the rewards are commonly small; and also he ought not to believe a report made to him through flattery. To this purpose the philosopher Hermes declares: "A reporter—or prevaricator of news—for either he lies to the one to whom he reports it, or he is false to him about whom he relays it."

Allegory
Coronis, who should not be killed, we shall understand as our soul, which we should not kill through sin, but instead guard it well. And St. Augustine says that the soul ought to be kept as a chest which is full of treasure, as the castle which is besieged by enemies, and the king who rests in his room of retreat. And this room ought to be closed in its five doors, which are the five senses of nature; and it is not any other thing to close these doors than to withdraw from the pleasures of the five senses.

And if it happens that the soul need to go forth through these doors to foreign operations, it ought to go forth measurable and wisely and in discretion, and also as the princes when they desire to go out of the rooms, when they have ushers before them holding scepters of office to make the way in the press. Also, when the soul needs to go forth to see, hear and speak and feel, it ought to have fear of the usher, who should have for Mass consideration of the pain of hell and the judgment of God. And to guard his soul thus, the sage admonishes: "With [all] watchfulness keep thy heart, because life issueth out from it." Proverbs 4[:23]

49 Juno

Text

With Juno do not preoccupy yourself too much;
If the nut be better than the shell,
Desire to have honor,
For better it is to value prowess than property.

Gloss

Juno is the goddess of riches, according to the fables of the poets. And because to have riches it is necessary to have and to acquire with great business and work, so that such business may distract from acquiring honor, and as honor and worthiness are more laudable than riches, inasmuch as the nut is better than the shell, it is said to the good knight that he should not so set his thought and happiness that worthiness is abandoned in its pursuit. To this purpose Hermes says that it is better to have poverty in doing good works than riches acquired easily, for worth is everlasting, and riches, vain and fallible.

Allegory

Juno, with whom (it is said) he ought not to preoccupy himself too much, who is taken for riches, we may thereby understand that the good spirit should devalue riches. And St. Bernard declares: "O son of Adam, covetous line, by which reason do you love so much worldly riches, which are neither true nor yours; and, whether you wish or not, at your death you must leave them?" And the Gospel says that the camel may pass more easily through the eye of a needle than the rich man enter into the kingdom of heaven, for the camel has only one hump on his back, but the evil rich man has two, one of worldly possessions and the other of sin. It is necessary that he leave the first hump at his death, but the other, whether he wishes or no, he will bear with him, unless he leave it before he die. To this purpose says our Lord in the Gospel: "It is easier for a camel to pass through the eye of a needle, than for a rich man to enter into the kingdom of heaven." Matthew 19[:24]

50 Amphiaraus

Text
Against the counsel of Amphiaraus
Do not go to destroy the city of Thebes
Or of Argos, or you will die;
Do not assemble a host with shield or targe.

Gloss
Amphiaraus was a very wise clerk of the city of Argos and displayed much learning.[1] When the king Adrastus wished to go to Thebes to destroy the city, Amphiaraus, who knew through his skill what harm might ensue because of it, said to the king that he should not go; and if he should go, all would be dead and destroyed. But he was not believed; so it happened as he said. For this wishes to say to the good knight that he should not undertake any great adventure against the counsel of the sages. But as Solomon declares: "The counsel of the sage profits little him who does not wish to use it."[2]

Allegory
By the counsel of Amphiaraus, against the which one ought not to go into battle, we can note that the good spirit ought to follow the saints' preachings. And St. Gregory says in the *Homilies*[3] that, just as the life of the body cannot be sustained without taking physical refreshment, so also the life of the soul cannot be sustained without often hearing the Word of God. Then receive the words of God, which you hear with literal ears, in your heart, for, when the word is not heard or retained in the stomach of memory, it is like the sick stomach when it throws up food; and thus entirely like the one who despairs in life about him who never retains but throws out everything, hence is the soul in peril of everlasting death that hears preachings and neither retains them nor ever follows them. Therefore the Holy Scripture says: "Man does not live in bread alone, but in every word that proceeds from the mouth of God." Matthew 4[:4]

51 Saturn the Saturnine

Text
Let your tongue be saturnine;[4]
Never be a bad neighbor to anyone.
To talk too much is a foul habit,
And he who has done so points to madness within.

---

1 *Science*: technical knowledge, that requiring study, in this case, astrology.
2 The exact citation has not been identified.
3 *Homilies on the Evangelists* 1.4.
4 *Saturnine*: tacitum, slow, heavy. See also Fable 8.

Gloss

Saturn, as I have said before, is a planet slow and sluggish. For this says to the good knight that his tongue ought to resemble it [Saturn]: for the tongue ought to be sluggish in that it does not talk too much; and wise, so that it does not misspeak of anyone, or of a matter from which one might derive presumption of folly. For a poet says, "By the word men know the wise man, and by the gaze the fool."[1]

Allegory

The tongue, which ought to be saturnine, is, on understanding, slow to speak. Hugh of St. Victor[2] says to this purpose that the mouth which does not guard against discretion is also like the city which is without a wall, like the vessel which has no bottom, like the horse which has no bridle, like the ship which is without rudder. The tongue ill-guarded glides like the eel, pierces like an arrow, reduces friends and multiplies enemies; it excites quarrels and disseminates discord; with one blow it beats and kills several persons. Who guards his tongue, guards his soul, for death and life are in the power of the tongue. To this purpose said David in his Psalter: "Who is the man that desires life: who loveth to see good days? Keep thy tongue from evil, and thy lips from speaking guile." Psalms 33[:13-14].

52 Apollo's Crow

Text

Believe the crow and his counsel;
Never be quick while
Bringing some bad news;
Safer it is in desisting.

Gloss

The crow,[3] so says the fable, encountered the raven[4] when he [the raven] carried the news to Phoebus about [the god's] beloved Coronis who had done ill, and she [the crow] pressed him so much that he [the raven] told her the reason for her [Coronis's] error. But she [the crow] dissuaded him from going by giving him the example of herself, who for a similar case had been chased out of the house of Pallas, where she had become accustomed to be greatly advanced.[5] But he would not believe her, for the which harm ensued to him. For this reason it is said to the good knight

---

1 The exact citation has not been identified.
2 Also attributed to Hugh of St. Victor in Christine's *Book of Human Integrity*.
3 *La corneille*, "she."
4 *Le corbel*, "he" (Christine is drawing an analogy between Coronis's misdeed and the crow's).
5 See Ovid, *Metamorphoses* 2.542.

that he ought to believe the crow. And Plato says: "Do not be a jangler, nor a great reporter of news to the king."

Allegory

That the crow ought to be believed is to say that the good spirit should use some counsel. As St. Gregory says in his *Morals*,[1] strength never succeeds where counsel does not exist, for strength is most quickly overthrown if it is not founded upon the gift of counsel; and the soul, which has lost inside itself the siege of counsel, on the outside is torn apart by diverse desires. Therefore the wise one says, "If wisdom shall enter into thy heart, counsel shall keep thee, and prudence shall preserve thee." Proverbs 2[:10-11].[2]

53 Ganymedes

Text

If you strive with one stronger than yourself
In playing several games of might,
Withdraw so that you will not be hurt.
Remember Ganymedes.

Gloss

Ganymedes[3] was a young gentleman of the Trojan line, and a fable declares that Phoebus and he strove together one day in casting a bar of iron. And, when Ganymedes could not withstand the strength of Phoebus, he was killed by the rebounding of the bar which Phoebus had launched so high that he lost sight of it. And therefore it is said that strife with one stronger and mightier than oneself is not good, for one may reach for himself no drawback. So says the wise man: "To sport with men who use ungracious games is a sign of pride, and ends commonly in anger."

Allegory

And when it is said that against the one stronger than himself he ought not to strive, it is to understand that the good spirit ought not to undertake too great a penance without counsel. St. Gregory says in his *Morals* [20.41] that penance does not benefit if it is not discreet; nor is the virtue of abstinence worth anything, if it is not so prescribed that it is harsher than the body may suffer. And for this concludes that no person ought to undertake without counsel from one more discreet than himself. For this says the wise man in his Proverbs [24.6]: "There shall be safety where there are many counsels," and the common proverb, "Do everything with some plan, and afterwards you will not regret it."

---

1 Book 5, but see also *Homilies, PL* 76:1017.
2 Christine omits "and knowledge please thy soul," the second half of verse 10.
3 Hyacinthus, not Ganymedes, in fact was slain; in Christine's source (the *Ovide moralisé*) the tale of Jacinthus (10.753-882, 3425-3519) follows that of Ganimeden (10.724-52 and 3362-3424).

54 Jason

Text

Do not resemble Jason,
Who through Medea won
The fleece of gold, for which afterwards he rendered to her
Very evil recompense and payment

Gloss

Jason was a knight of Greece, who went into a strange country, that is to say, in the isle of Colchos, through the urging of Peleus, his uncle, who from envy desired his death. The one had a sheep who had golden fleece and through enchantment was guarded, but as the conquest was so strong, no one came there who did not lose his life. Medea, who was the daughter of the king of this country, took such great love to Jason that by means of the enchantments which she knew, of which she was sovereign mistress, gave charms and took enchantments to Jason, through which he won the golden fleece; by which he received honor above all living knights, and was restored from death by Medea, with whom he had promised to be loyal friends all their days. But after he broke faith, and loved another, and entirely abandoned and relinquished her, even though she was of sovereign beauty. For this says to the good knight that he ought not resemble Jason, who displayed ingratitude and disloyalty to the one who had done to him too much good. Therefore it is a villainous thing for any noble to be ungrateful and ignorant of any good, if he has received any from a lady, gentlewoman, or another person; for all his days he ought to remember it and provide recompense in his power. To this purpose says Hermes: "Do not be slow nor delaying in repaying him who has done well to you, for you ought to remember it all your days."

Allegory

The good spirit should not resemble Jason, who was ungrateful and who for benefits received from his creator ought not to be ungrateful. And St. Bernard says on the Songs of Songs that ingratitude is an enemy to the soul, a destroyer of virtues, dispersion of merits, loss of benefits. Ingratitude is also like a dry wind, which dries up the fountain of pity, the dew of grace, and the river of mercy. To this purpose says the sage: "For the hope of the unthankful shall melt away as the winter's ice, and shall run off an unprofitable water." Wisdom 16[:29]

55 Gorgon

Text

Guard yourself against the serpent Gorgon;
Guard well that you do not look at her;[1]
Hold remembrance of Perseus,
He will tell you the whole story.

Gloss

Gorgon, so says a fable, was a gentlewoman of sovereign beauty. But because Phoebus[2] dallied with her in the temple of Diana, the goddess was so enraged that she transformed her into a serpent[3] of very horrible shape; and this serpent had such a power that all men who looked at her became suddenly changed to stone. And for the evil which ensued from her, Perseus, the valiant knight, journeyed to battle with the fierce beast; and in the gleam of his shield, which was made entirely of gold, he beheld himself so as not to look at the evil serpent;[4] and he did so entirely that he severed her head.

Many an exposition can be made from this fable, and the Gorgon can be understood as a city or town which formerly used to enjoy great bounty; but, through the vices of the inhabitants, it became a serpent and venomous, that is to say, that it did much harm to their neighbors in the marshes, as in entirely robbing and pillaging, and the merchants and others passing by were taken and held and sent to a destroyed prison, and thus were they changed into stone. Perseus saw himself reflected in his shield, that is to say, in strength and chivalry, and journeyed to fight against that city and took it and took the power from it to do greater evil. And therefore a very beautiful lady but of wicked dealings might exist, who, through her covetousness, deprives many of what they own. And several other understandings may be taken from this. For this intends to say to the good knight that he guard himself well from gazing at evil things, which might attract him to evil. And Aristotle says: "Flee people full of iniquity; and follow wise men and study in their books and gaze at yourself in their deeds."

Allegory

That the Gorgon you should not behold, or think of for whatever pleasures, but behold yourself in the shield of the state of perfection and flee from what vices do. Chrysostomus declares that, as it is impossible that fire burn in water, also it is impossible that compunction[5] of heart exist among the pleasure of the world; they are two contrary things and

---

1 Christine is punning on *gardes* (guard) and *regardes* (look at) because of the paralyzing power of Medusa's gaze.
2 Neptune raped her instead of Phoebus in Ovid, *Met.* 4.797.
3 In Ovid, only her hair metamorphoses into snakes.
4 In Ovid, Perseus sees her reflection in the shield, which saves him.
5 The prick of conscience, or contrition.

will destroy, one the other, for compunction is the mother of tears and pleasures engender laughter; compunction restrains the heart and pleasure enlarges it. To this purpose says Scripture, "They that sow in tears shall reap in joy." [Psalms 125:5]

56 Mars and Venus

Text
If lovers shorten the night for you,
Watch that Phoebus does not harm you,
Through which you may be taken
In Vulcan's bonds and surprised.

Gloss
A fable says that Mars and Venus loved each other as paramours. One night arrived when the two lovers were asleep arm in arm. Phoebus, who sees clearly, surprised and caught sight of them; to Vulcan, husband of Venus, he accused them. Then he [Vulcan] who saw them in that plight forged a bond and a chain of brass and bound them together, the two entirely, so that they could not move, and as he who is smith of the heavens can work subtly, therefore he surprised them, and afterwards went before the other gods and showed them his shame. And the fable says that such a one who riots there, who might well fall into a similar misdeed, becomes entangled.[1] To this fable diverse expositions may be set, and it may quite sovereignly touch on some points of astrology for those who can subtly understand it. But to our purpose it says that the good knight should watch that in such a case he is not surprised by having forgotten. And a wise man says: "Scarcely exists the thing so secret that it can be perceived by no one."

Allegory
There where the authority says: "Lovers shorten the night for you," we shall say that the good spirit ought to guard itself against the watches of the Enemy. To this the pope St. Leo says that the ancient enemy, who transfigured himself into an angel of light, ceases not to set all the snares of his temptations and to spy how he hopes to corrupt the faith of the believers; he gazes at him whom he will embrace with the fire of covetousness, whom he will inflame with the ardor of lechery, to whom he will propose the seductions of gluttony; he examines the customs of everything, examines hearts, conjectures affections, and where he finds the creature most inclined, most frivolous and busy, he there seeks to cause harm. For this reason says St. Peter: "Be sober and watch: because your adversary the devil, as a roaring lion, goeth about seeking whom he may devour." 2 Peter last chapter [1 Peter 5:8]

---

1 Meaning "confused," but Christine is also playing with the image of the nets of Vulcan.

57 Thamaris

Text

Do not dispraise Thamaris,
For although she is a woman, you recall
The passage where Cyrus was taken,
For dearly he bought the dispraise.

Gloss

Thamaris was queen of Amazonia, a very valiant lady, full of great prowess, of great hardiness and wisdom in arms and government. Cyrus, the great king of Persia, who had conquered many a region with a great host, moved to go against the realm of Amazonia, of which he estimated the strength as very little. But this one, who was expert and subtle in the craft of arms, suffered him to enter into her realm without killing him, until he was caught in the narrow passage between mountains, where the country was very rough. Then through the ambushes of Thamaris Cyrus was assailed in every part of the host by the women and was brought so much forth that he was taken, and his people all dead and taken. The queen had him brought before her and had his head cut off and thrown into a tub full of the blood of his barons, whom she had beheaded in his presence. To him Thamaris spoke in such a manner: "Cyrus, who never had enough of human blood, now you may drink your fill." And thus ended Cyrus, the great king of Persia, who never before had been overcome in any battle. Therefore it is said to the good knight that he should never be so overweening that he has no doubt that a mishap might befall him through some fortune and through the lesser in him. To this purpose Plato says: "Do not dispraise anyone for his small faculty, for his virtues may be great."

Allegory

Thamaris, who should not be dispraised for all that she was a woman, means that the good spirit should not dispraise her nor hate the state of humility, be it in religion or another state, and that humility invites praise. John Cassian says that in no way may the edifice of virtues in our soul be raised or erected itself, if first the foundations of true humility are not first tasted in our heart, the which, set very steadfastly, may sustain the loftiness of perfection and charity. Therefore the sage declares: "The greater thou art, the more humble thyself in all things, and thou shalt find grace before God." Ecclesiasticus 3[:30]

58 Medea

Text

Do not allow your sense to miscarry
With foolish delight, or to remove

Your goods, if it be asked
Of you; and look at Medea.

Gloss

Medea was one of the most knowing women of sorcery who ever lived and who had the most knowledge, according to that which the stories relay. And notwithstanding that she allowed her sense to miscarry to her own will to fulfill her delight, when she allowed herself to be mastered by foolish love, so that on Jason she set her heart and gave honor to him, body and goods; for which afterward to him she rendered an evil reward. Therefore it is said that the good knight should not allow himself to overcome reason with foolish delight in whatever situation, if he wishes to employ the virtue of strength. And Plato declares: "A man of light heart is soon annoyed by that which he loves."

Allegory

That he should not allow his sense to miscarry with foolish delight may be understood that the good spirit should not allow his own will to be mastered; for if the mastery of individual will does not cease, there will be no hell, nor will the fire of hell ever have mastery except over the person who allows his own will to be lord, for individual will fights against God and is proud; it is that which strips paradise and clothes hell and voids the value of the blood of Jesus Christ and submits the world to the servitude of the Adversary. To this purpose the sage declares: "The rod and reproof give wisdom: but the child that is left to his own will bringeth his mother to shame." Proverbs 29[:15]

59 Galathea

Text

If you are subject to the god Cupid,
Keep yourself from the enraged giant,
So that the rock may not be pushed
On Acis and Galathea.

Gloss

Galathea was a nymph or a goddess who loved a young man named Acis. A giant of ugly shape was enamored of Galathea, who did not deign to love him; and he spied on them so completely that he perceived the two of them in the crevice of a rock; then he became overlaid with sudden rage, and the rock trembled in such a way that it completely crushed Acis. But Galathea, who was a nymph, dove into the sea and by this means escaped. This is to understand that the good knight keep himself in such a case from being surprised by such a one who has power and the will to injure him.

Allegory

That he should keep himself from the giant, who is given to Cupid, that is, that the good spirit keep himself so that he has no imagination of the world or of the things that belong to it, but has every day remembrance that all worldly things are of small endurance. And St. Jerome upon Jeremiah says that there exists nothing which ought to be reputed long among the things which will come to an end; not for anything is our time in comparison with everlasting eternity. To this purpose the sage declares: "those things are passed away like a shadow, and like a post that runneth on." Wisdom 5[:9]

60 Peleus[1]

Text

Flee the goddess of discord;
Evil are her lines and her cord.
She marred the marriage of Peleus
For which many a people afterwards assembled.

Gloss

Discord is a goddess of evil dealings. And a fable says that, when Peleus was married to the goddess Thetis, of which Achilles was born afterwards, Jupiter and all the gods and goddesses appeared at the nuptials, but the goddess of discord had never been summoned. And therefore envious of it she came without being asked; but she did not come for nothing, for she performed her duty there. When the three powerful goddesses, Pallas, Juno, Venus, were seated for dinner at a table, there came Lady Discord and threw on the table an apple of gold, on which had been written: "Let this be given to the most beautiful." Then the festivities were disrupted, for each argued that she ought to have it. They went before Jupiter to adjudicate this discord, but he would not please one to displease another. Therefore they put the debate before Paris of Troy, who then was a shepherd. When his mother had dreamed, while she had been pregnant with him, that he would be the cause of the destruction of Troy, he had then been sent to the forest of a shepherd, with whom he pretended to be son. And there Mercury, who conducted the ladies, told him [Paris] whose son he was; then he abandoned watching sheep and went to Troy to his great parents. Thus the fable testifies, where the true story is hidden under poetic cover; and because often many a great mischief has happened, and befalling through discord and debate, indicates to the good knight that he ought to guard himself against discord, in that it is a very ugly custom to be discordant and to instigate riots. Pythagoras says: "Do not travel on the road where enmities grow."

---

1 See also Fable 73.

Allegory
As it is said that discord should be fled, so also the good spirit should flee all hindrances of conscience and contentions, and shun riots. Cassiodorus on the Psalter says: "Chiefly," he declares, "flee contentions and riots, for to contend against peace is madness; to contend against his sovereign, that is folly; to contend against his subject, that is great villainy." Therefore St. Paul declares: "Not in contention and envy." St. Paul to the Romans 13[:13]

61 The Death of Laomedon[1]

Text
Never forget the misdeed
If you have done so against anyone,
For he will well keep the reward for you.
For it Laomedon was destroyed.

Gloss
Laomedon, as I have said before, was king of Troy; and he had committed great villainy against the Greek barons to drive them from his country, the which they never forgot. But Laomedon had forgotten it when the Greeks ran against him, who surprised him unprepared, so they destroyed and killed him. Therefore it is said to the good knight that, if he has acted badly against someone, that he be on his guard, for he may be sure that it will not be forgotten, but instead avenged, whenever he may, in time and in place. And to this purpose Hermes says: "Watch that your enemies do not surprise you unprepared."

Allegory
That he should not forget the misdeed, if he has done so to another, may be understood as, when the good spirit fails himself in sin through fault of resistance, he should think that he will be punished for it, is the one damned by it, unless he amends himself. And about that St. Gregory declares that the justice of God now goes beautifully and at a slow pace, but in time to come it will recompense more grievously; the mercy of God will be tardy in his expectation. To this purpose the prophet Joel declares: "Turn to the Lord your God: for he is gracious and merciful, patient and rich in mercy, and ready to repent of the evil." Joel [2:13]

62 Semele

Text
If it happens that you are maddened by love,
Watch at the least to whom you speak.
That your doings may not be troubled,
Remind yourself of Semele.

---

1 See also Fable 37.

Gloss

The fable relays that Semele was a gentlewoman whom Jupiter loved as a paramour. Juno, who was jealous, took the appearance of an ancient woman, came to Semele, and through beautiful words began to reason with her and so much that Semele made known to her all the love of her and her lover; and she boasted about being well loved and well delighted by him. Then the goddess said to her, who took no keep of the deceit, so that she perceived nothing again about the love, that when she would be with him again, she request of him a gift; and when she will have well requested of him and accorded, that she ask of him that he promise to embrace her in the same manner as he embraced Juno, his wife, when he wished to take pleasure with her; and through this manner she would be able to perceive the love of her lover. Semele did not forget, and when she had made the request of Jupiter, who had promised her, and, as god, could not repeal it, because of it became very sad and well knew that she had been deceived. Then Jupiter assumed the appearance of fire and embraced his beloved, who in a short time was scorched and burned, for which Jupiter had great heaviness about the adventure. Of this fable may be taken various interpretations, and especially about the science of astronomy, as the masters say. But it may be that in some way a gentlewoman was deceived by the wife of her lover, whereupon he made her die through inadvertence. And therefore it is said to the good knight that he should watch himself when he speaks of a matter that he wishes to hide, before he plans his words and to whom he says it and what he says, for through these circumstances the matters may be understood. Therefore Hermes declares: "Do not reveal the secrets of your thoughts except to those whom you have well proven."

Allegory

That he should watch to whom he speaks, we may understand that the good spirit, whatever his thoughts may be, should watch himself in every situation where evil suspicion may fall to another. As St. Augustine says in the *Book of Sheep* that we ought not only to take care about having a good conscience, but inasmuch as our infirmity may, and as much as the diligence of human frailty may, we ought to take care that we do nothing which enhances an evil suspicion to our steadfast brothers. About these words, St. Paul remarks, "In all things shew thyself an example of good works." Titus 2[:7]

63 Diana[1]

Text
Do not trust too much the pleasure
Of Diana, for it is not fitting

---

1 See also Fables 23 and 69 on Diana.

To those pursuing chivalry
To amuse themselves in hunting.

Gloss

Diana is named goddess of the woods and of hunting; so it is said to the good knight pursuing the exalted name of arms that he should not amuse himself too much in pleasure of hunting, for it is a thing that tends to idleness. And Aristotle says that idleness leads to all inconveniences.

Allegory

That the pleasure of Diana ought not to be followed too much, which is said for idleness, the good spirit may note the same and that it is to avoid. St. Gregory declares: "Every day do some work of good, to the extent that the Adversary may find you always occupied in some good exhortation." To this purpose it is said about the wise woman: "She hath looked well to the paths of her house, and hath not eaten her bread idle." Proverbs 31[:27]

64 Arachne

Text

Do not boast; for evil followed from it
To Arachne, who misgauged so totally
That against Pallas she boasted,
For which the goddess enchanted her.

Gloss

Arachne, this fable says, was a gentlewoman very skilled in the art of weaving and spinning, but was too overweening in her wisdom, and indeed she boasted to Pallas, for which the goddess was angry with her, so that for this boasting she changed her into a spider. And said: "Because you have boasted so much of spinning and weaving, hereafter for all your days you shall spin and weave work of no value." And truly from this came the spiders, who never cease to spin and weave. So it may be that someone boasted to her mistress, for which evil ensued to her in some manner. Therefore it is said to the good knight that he should not boast, as it may be a very easy thing for a knight to be boastful, and it may abuse too much the reputation of his goodness. And similarly Plato declares: "When you do a thing better than another, watch that you do not boast of it, for your worth by it will be much the less."

Allegory

That he ought not to boast, we may say that the good spirit guards himself from boasting. For against boasting St. Augustine states in the twelfth book [:8] of *The City of God* that boasting is not a vice of human praising, but a vice of the perverse soul, which loves human praising and despises the true testimony of correct conscience. To this purpose the sage declares: "What hath pride profited us? or what advantage hath the boasting of riches brought us?" Wisdom 5[:8]

65 Adonis

Text

If too great a desire you pursue
In loving excessively the pleasure of hunting,
Of Adonis be mindful at the least,
Who was killed by the wild pig boar.

Gloss

Adonis was a very gallant gentleman and of great beauty. Venus loved him as a lover, but because he delighted too much in hunting, Venus, who feared that harm would come to him through some misadventure, begged him many a time that he would take care in hunting the great beast. But Adonis never wished to do so, thus he was killed by a wild pig. Therefore it is said to the good knight that if he would hunt to every finish, then he should take care in such a hunt lest harm may come to him. To this purpose Sedechias the prophet declares that a king should not allow his son too much use of the hunt or of idleness, but he should make him informed of good conditions and to flee vanities.

Allegory

That of Adonis he should be mindful may be understood that, if the good spirit is in some way deviated, that at the least he should be mindful of the great peril of perseverance. For, as the Adversary has great power over sinners, St. Peter says in the Second Epistle [2:19] that sinners are servants[1] of corruption and the Adversary has power over them, for he who is surmounted by another in battle is become his serf. And in sign of this it is said in the Apocalypse: "And power was given him over every tribe, and people." Apocalypse 13[:7]

66 The First Troy

Text

If it should happen that enemies assail you,
Beware that you and your people do not rise up
Against them, so that your city empties;
Take example from the first Troy.

Gloss

When Hercules with a great abundance of Greeks came against the first Troy and the king Laomedon had heard told of their coming, then he with all the people that he might have in the city surged together outside and went against them to the riverside. And there they assembled with very fierce battle, and the city was left emptied of people. Then Ajax

---

1 Also serfs, with the feudal meaning.

Telamonius, who had hidden with a great host behind the walls of the city, immobilized it, and then was the first Troy taken. Therefore it is said to the good knight he watch that through such a trick he is not deceived by his enemies. And Hermes says: "Guard yourself against the artifice of your enemies."

Allegory

That he should guard himself lest his enemies assail him, so that his city is not emptied, it means that the good spirit should every day hold himself seized and filled with virtues. And about this St. Augustine declares that, just as when in time of war the men of arms never take off their arms nor strip them off, whether day or night, so also during the time of present life, he should not be despoiled of virtues, for he whom the Adversary finds without virtues is also like him whom the Adversary has found without arms. Therefore says the Gospel: "A strong man armed keepeth his court." [Luke 11:21]

67 Orpheus[1]

Text

Do not besot yourself with the lyre
Of Orpheus, if you wish to choose
Arms as a principal profession.
To follow instruments you do not need a craft.

Gloss

Orpheus was a poet; and the fable says that he knew how to play the lyre so well that everything—the running waters in returning on their course, and the birds of the air, the savage beasts and the fierce serpent, in remembering their cruelty—similarly stopped to listen to the melody of the lyre. This is to understand that he played so well that all people, of whatever condition that they may be, delighted in hearing the poet play. And because such instruments frequently besot the hearts of men, it is said to the good knight that he should not delight in it too much, as it is not fitting to the sons of chivalry to amuse themselves on instruments, nor in other idleness. To this purpose declares an authority: "The melody of the instrument is the snare of the serpent." And Plato states: "He who sets his pleasure wholly in carnal delights is more of a serf[2] than a slave."

Allegory

The lyre of Orpheus, with which he should not be besotted, we may take that the chivalrous spirit should not be besotted or amused in whatever worldly company, whether they be relatives of others. St. Augustine says, in the book of *The Singularity of Clerics*, that the solitary man who never associates with the company of the voluptuous is stimu-

1 See also Fable 70, on Orpheus and Eurydice.
2 "Serf" meaning more contractually bound than a literally bound slave.

lated less by the prickings of the flesh, and they who never see the riches of the world feel less the torments of avarice. Therefore David remarks: "I have watched and am become as a sparrow all alone on the housetop." [Psalm 101:8]

68 Paris

Text

Do not found on a prophetic dream,
Nor upon a foolish illusion
A great enterprise, whether it be right or wrong,
And hold remembrance of Paris.

Gloss

Because Paris had dreamed that in Greece he would ravish Helen, a great army was created and sent from Troy into Greece, where Paris ravished Helen. Then for that wrongful deed all the power of Greece came to amend it against Troy, which was then such a great country that it extended as far as the country that we call Apulia and Calabria in Italy, and at that time was named Little Greece.[1] And among them were Achilles and the Myrmidons, who were such valiant combatants; this great quantity of people confounded Troy and all the country. Therefore it is said to the good knight that upon a prophetic dream he should undertake to create no important thing, for immense harm and difficulty may come of it. And that a great enterprise should not be made without great deliberation of counsel, Plato declares: "Do nothing unless your sense has beforehand considered it."

Allegory

That a great project should not be founded upon a prophetic dream means that the good spirit should never presume nor raise himself in arrogance for whatever grace that God may give to him. And St. Gregory says in the *Morals* that four species exist in which all of the swelling of arrogance is demonstrated. The first, that when they have the good, they reckon that they have it from themselves; the second when the good that they have, they imagine to have well deserved and received it through their merits; the third when they boast of having the good that they never had; the fourth when they despise others and desire that the one know the good that is in them. Against this vice speaks the sage in Proverbs: "I hate arrogance, and pride, and every wicked way, and a mouth with a double tongue." Proverbs 8[:13]

---

1 Apulia and Calabria are two provinces in the southern portion of Italy with Greek ruins remaining even today. St. Jerome called the region "Magna Graecia," Great Greece.

69 Actaeon

Text

If you love well dogs and birds,
Actaeon, the gentlest of gentlemen,
Who became a stag, remember well,
And watch that some similar thing does not befall you.

Gloss

Actaeon was a gentleman very courteous and of gentle condition, and loved dogs and birds too much. And the fable says that one day he hunted all alone in a thick forest, where his men had lost track of him. Then because Diana, the goddess of the woods, had hunted in the forest until the hour of noon, so she was chafed and hot from the heat of the sun, so therefore she had the desire to bathe herself in a clear and beautiful fountain located there; and when she was entirely naked in the fountain, surrounded by nymphs and goddesses who served her, Actaeon, who took no heed, burst in upon her and saw the goddess entirely naked; the face of whom, for her great chastity, reddened out of shame and was very doleful. And then she said: "Because I know that young gentlemen will solely boast of ladies and gentlewomen, so that you cannot boast that you have seen me naked I shall take from you the power to speak." Then she cursed him; and suddenly Actaeon became an antlered stag, and nothing was left to him of his human form except understanding only. Then he, full of great sorrow and sudden fear, went fleeing through the bushes, and soon was pursued by his own dogs and called by the same men, who went searching for him through the forest; but now they have found him and they did not know him. There was Actaeon downed, who, before his men, wept a great gout, and willingly would have cried mercy to them if he could speak; and since then harts began to weep [at the moment of death]. Where Actaeon was killed and martyred in great sorrow by his own company,[1] who in a short while had entirely devoured him. Upon this fable may be made many diverse expositions, but to our purpose it may be that a young man who had abandoned everything to idleness, and had expended all that he had and his goods to the delight of his body and in pleasure of the hunt, and in keeping his retinue idle. By it may be said that he was hated by Diana, who signifies chastity, and devoured by his own retinue. Therefore it is said to the good knight that he keep himself from being destroyed in a like case. And a sage declares: "Idleness engenders ignorance and error."

---

1 Here *mesgnee*, referring to his own aristocratic retinue of men, servants, and dogs.

Allegory

Actaeon, who became a stag, we may understand as the true penitent who was often a sinner, now has vanquished his own flesh and made it serve the spirit and assumed the state of penitence. And St. Augustine says on the Psalter[1] that penitence is a very easy deed and a light burden; and it should not be named "deed" for the burdened man, but the wings of a bird flying, for, as the birds carry to earth the burden of their wings, and their wings carry them to the sky, so also, as we carry on earth the burden of penitence, it will carry us to the sky. To this purpose the Gospel declares: "Do penance: for the kingdom of heaven is at hand." Matthew 3[:2]

70 Orpheus and Eurydice

Text

Do not go to the gates of iron
To seek Eurydice in hell;
For a little while Orpheus played his lyre there
For everyone, as I have heard told.

Gloss

Of Orpheus the poet, who harped so well, a fable tells that he was married to the beautiful Eurydice, but the day of the nuptials she went disporting herself in a meadow barefoot because of the great heat of the sun. A shepherd coveted the beauty and ran around to ravish her, and when she fled before him out of fear of him, she was bitten by a snake which was hidden under the grass, after which the maiden was dead in a short time. Orpheus was exceedingly sad from this harmful mishap. So he took his lyre and went to the gates of iron in the shadowy valley in front of the infernal palace, and then he began to harp a piteous lay, and so sweetly he sang that all the tormented of hell became calm and all the infernal offices ceased in order to listen to the melody of the lyre; and especially Proserpina, the goddess of hell, was moved by great pity. Then Pluto, Lucifer, Cerberus, and Acharon, who because of the harper saw the offices relinquish the infernal pains, rendered to him his wife on condition that he go before and she after, without him turning around behind (for if he turned around, he would lose her) until they were past the infernal valley. On this condition Eurydice was rendered up to him again. So Orpheus went before and his beloved after; but he, who loved excessively, could not keep from turning around for his beloved, whom he desired to look at; and all of a sudden Eurydice departed from him and was again in hell, nor might he have her again. This fable may be understood in many ways. And it may be that some man had lost his wife taken from him and later returned and later still lost her again. Or it may be said that who seeks well Eurydice in hell seeks an impossible thing; and though he not recover her, it should

1 Actually, in *Sermon 164*, in *PL* 38:898.

not cause melancholy. Solomon says the same: "It is folly to seek that which it is impossible to have."

Allegory

That he should not go to seek Eurydice in hell, we may understand that the good spirit ought not to ask or request of God a thing miraculous and marvelous, which is called tempting God. And St. Augustine declares, on the Gospel of St. John, that the request that the creature makes of God is not fulfilled when she requests a thing which may not be done, or which ought not to be done, or a thing which she would use poorly if it were granted to her, or a thing which could wound her soul if it were granted. And therefore it derives from the mercy of God when he does give a creature a thing which he knows that she would use badly. To this purpose St. James the Apostle declares in his Epistle: "You ask, and receive not; because you ask amiss." St. James 4[:3]

71 Achilles

Text

If you would truly recognize knights
And enclose them in a cloister,
The attempt that was made on Achilles
Will teach you to identify them.

Gloss

Achilles, so says a fable, was son of the goddess Thetis, and because she knew, as a goddess, that if her son used arms, he would die, she, who loved too greatly with a great passion, hid him in the garments of a maiden and made him wear a veil like a nun; in the abbey of the goddess Vesta for a long time Achilles was hidden, until he had sufficiently matured. And the fable declares that he engendered Pyrrhus, who was very chivalrous, on the daughter of the king Hysirus.[1] Then began the great Trojan wars, and the Greeks divined through their oracles that it was necessary for them to have Achilles; he was sought everywhere, but news of him could not be heard. Ulysses, who was too full of great malice and who searched for him everywhere, came to the temple, but when he could not perceive the truth, thought with great malice and subtlety. Then Ulysses took rings, wimples, belts, and all kinds of jewels of ladies, and with this, arms of knights, beautiful and bright, and threw everything down in the middle of the palace in the presence of the ladies, and said that each should take that which pleased them most. And then, as each thing is drawn to its nature, the ladies ran to the jewels and Achilles seized the arms; and then Ulysses ran to embrace him and said that he was that which he sought. And because knights should be more inclined to arms than to pretty ornaments, which

---

1 This name has not been identified. Other manuscripts do not name the king; in the ancient stories and tradition, his name is Lycomedes.

appertain to ladies, the authority would say that by this one may recognize the true knight. To this purpose Leginon declares: "The knight is not known except by arms." And Hermes states: "Know men before you have completed an engagement."

Allegory

Where it is said, "If you would truly recognize knights," we may take that the knight Jesus Christ should be known through the arms of good transactions, and that such a knight has the praise due to the good. St. Jerome says in an *Epistle* that just as the justice of God does not leave any evil unpunished, so also it does not leave any good unrewarded; so then to good people no work should seem hard, nor time long, when they await everlasting glory as reward. Therefore Holy Scripture declares: "Do you therefore take courage, and let not your hands be weakened: for there shall be a reward for your work." 2 Paralipomenon 15[:7]

72 Atalanta

Text

Do not compete with Atalanta,
For she has a greater talent than you
In forceful running, which is her craft;
Of such running you have no need.

Gloss

Atalanta was a nymph of great beauty, but her destiny was diverse, in that because of her, several lost their lives. This gentlewoman, because of her great beauty, was coveted by many to have in marriage. But such an edict was made that no one would have her if he did not defeat her in running; if she beat him, he had to die. Of marvelous swiftness was Atalanta, so that no one might overtake her in running, and on this path many died. This running may be understood in several manners. And it may be something much coveted by many, but without great work no one may have her; the running that she does, it is the defense or resistance of the thing. And similarly may be noted the fable in which several make great contest without need. Thus the authority intends to say that a man hardy and courageous should not challenge him to compete too much over useless things, which are not touching his honor, nor of which may he choose him; for many great injuries exist many a time following such strife. And Thesille declares: "You should do whatever is more profitable to the body and more fitting to the soul, and avoid the contrary."

Allegory

"Do not compete with Atalanta," we may understand that the good spirit should never hinder a thing which the world does, or in whatever government it may be. And about this St. Augustine in an *Epistle*[1] says that the world is more perilous when it is safe for creatures than when it is harsh; but the more he sees it disagreeable, the less it ought to hinder him, and the less when it attracts his love than when it gives occasion to be despised. To this purpose St. John the Evangelist declares in his first Epistle: "If any man love the world, the charity of the Father is not in him." 1 John 2[:15]

73 The Judgment of Paris[2]

Text
Do not judge as Paris did,
For one receives many a hard return
For approving bad sentences,
For which many have had bad reward.

Gloss
The fable says that the three goddesses of great power, which is to understand, Pallas, goddess of wisdom, Juno, goddess of possessions, and Venus, goddess of love, came before Paris holding an apple of gold, which said: "Let this be given to the most beautiful and most powerful." About this apple there was great discord, for each said that she ought to have it, and when they were sent to Paris because of this discord, Paris diligently tried to discover the strength and power of each of them by himself. Then Pallas said: "I am goddess of chivalry and of wisdom, and through me are dispensed arms of the knights and the sciences of the clerks; and if you would give me the apple, you know that I will make you chivalrous over all and you will surpass all others in every science." After that Juno, goddess of possessions and of mastery, declared: "Through me are dispensed the great treasures of the world; and if you would give me the apple, I will make you more rich and powerful than any other." After that Venus spoke with many amorous words and said: "I am she who keeps school in love and in gaiety, and who makes fools to be wise and sages to act like a fool; and the rich, the poor, and the exiled, enriched. There is no power that can be compared with mine. And if you would give me the apple, the love of the beautiful Helen of Greece you will be given through me, which may serve you better than whatever riches may do." And then Paris gave his sentence and renounced chivalry and wisdom and riches for Venus, to whom he gave the apple, for which judgment Troy was later destroyed. This is to understand that, because Paris was not chivalrous, nor preoccupied much by riches for him, but in love all his thoughts remained, is understood that to Venus he gave the apple of gold. And therefore it is said to the good knight that he should not act similarly. And

---

1 In *Epistle 145* to Anastasius (*PL* 33:593).
2 See also Fable 60.

Pythagoras says: "The judge who does not judge justly deserves every evil."

Allegory

Paris who judged foolishly means that the good spirit should beware of making judgment about others. About this speaks St. Augustine against the Manicheans, that there exist two things which we in especial should avoid: judgment about others primarily, for we do not know with what disposition things are accomplished, the which to condemn it is great presumption, for we should interpret them in a better light; secondly, for we are not certain what those will be who at present are good or evil. To this purpose says our Lord in the Gospel: "Judge not, that you may not be judged. For with what judgment you judge, you shall be judged." Matthew 7[:1-2]

74 Fortune

Text

In Fortune, the great goddess,
Do not trust, nor in her promise;
For in a little while she changes herself,
The most exalted she often throws into the mire.

Gloss

Fortune, according to the manner of speaking of the poets, may be well named the great goddess, for through her we see governed the course of worldly things. And because she promises enough prosperity to many, and, indeed, gives it to some and in a little while takes it back as she pleases, indicates to the good knight he should not trust in her promises or be discomforted by his adversaries. And Socrates says: "The turns of Fortune are like engines."

Allegory

By this, when he says that he should not trust in Fortune, we may understand that the good spirit should flee and despise the delights of the world. About this Boethius declares in his third book of *Consolation*[1] that the happiness of the Epicureans should be named unhappiness, for it is the true, full, and perfect happiness which may make man sufficiently mighty, reverend, solemn and joyous, the which additions do not urge the things whereon the worldly people set their happiness. Therefore God declares through the prophet: "Oh my people, they that call thee blessed, the same deceive thee." Isaiah 3[:12]

---

1 Perhaps *The Consolation of Philosophy* 3 prose 2, according to Bühler's notes.

75 Paris the Warrior

Text

To undertake and advance war,
Do not act like Paris the beginner;
For he would understand better, I do not doubt it,
Amusing himself in the beautiful arms of his love.

Gloss

Paris was never conditioned to arms but wholly to love. And therefore it is said that the good knight should not make a captain of his host, or of his battles, a knight not trained in arms. And therefore Aristotle says to Alexander: "You should establish as constable for your chivalrous band from those whom you perceive as wise and expert in arms."

Allegory

That you do not use Paris to begin war, that is, that the good spirit, tending to the single chivalry of heaven, should be wholly withdrawn from the world and have chosen the contemplative life. And St. Gregory on Ezekiel says that the contemplative life is preferred by the good knight to the active life as the more worthy and greater, for the active life involves itself in the labor of the present life, but the contemplative life commences now so as to taste the flavor of the repose to come. And therefore of Mary Magdalene, in whom contemplation is figured, the Gospel declares: "Mary hath chosen the best part, which shall not be taken away from her." Luke 10[:42]

76 Cephalus

Text

Do not preoccupy yourself with spying on anyone,
But always go on your path.
Cephalus, or his javelin,
Will teach it to you, and the wife of Lot.

Gloss

Cephalus was an ancient knight, and a fable says that all his life he was much entertained by, and delighted in, the pleasure of the chase, and he knew marvelously well how to hurl a javelin that he had, which had such a property that it was never hurled in vain and always killed whatever it struck; and because he was accustomed to rise every morning and go into the forest to spy on the wild beast, his wife was in great jealousy over him from the suspicion that he was amorous with another besides her; and, to know the truth, went after him to spy. And Cephalus, who was in the woods, when he heard the leaves crackle where his wife had hidden, imagined that it was a wild beast, cast his javelin and struck his wife, and thus he killed her. Cephalus was sorrowful over this misadventure, but no remedy for it could be set. The wife of Lot, according to the testimony of

Holy Scripture, turned around, against the commandment of the angel, when she heard behind her the five cities melt, and for this was entirely transformed into a mass of salt. And as all such things are figured, it may be set many understandings. But, to take in the example of the truth, no good man should delight in spying on another in a matter which may not pertain to him. And as no one would wish to be spied upon, Hermes said: "Do nothing to your companion that you would not wish that he would do to you, and do not desire to set any snares in order take men, or purchase their injury through ambush or ruse, for at the last it will turn upon you."

Allegory

That he should not preoccupy himself with spying on anyone may be understood that the good spirit ought not to give pain in order to know the doings of another, or to inquire of news about another. And St. John Chrysostom on the Gospel of St. Matthew declares: "How," says he, "do you see in the deeds of another so many small shortcomings and in your own deeds allow to pass so many great shortcomings? If you love yourself better than your neighbor, why do you entrap his deeds and leave your own? Be first diligent in considering your actions, and then consider the actions of others." To this purpose our Lord in the Gospel says: "And why seest thou the mote that is in thy brother's eye; and seest not the beam that is in thy own eye?" Matthew 7[1:3]

77 Helenus

Text
Do not despise the counsel
Of Helenus; I counsel you so,
For often many an injury happens
Through not desiring to believe the sages.

Gloss
Helenus was brother of Hector and son of Priam, the king of Troy. He was a very wise clerk and full of knowledge. So he counseled, as much as he could, that Paris not go to Greece to ravish Helen; but he would not believe him, for which great harm befell the Trojans. Therefore it is said to the good knight that he should believe the sages and their counsel. And Hermes says: "Whoever honors the sages and uses their counsel is everlasting."

Allegory
Helenus, who counseled against the war, means that the good spirit should avoid temptations. And St. Jerome says that the sinner has no excuse that he leave off surmounting temptation, for the enemy tempter is so feeble that he may not overcome unless someone wishes to give himself to him. And about this says St. Paul the Apostle: "God is faithful, who will not suffer you to be tempted above that which you are able: but

will make also with temptation issue, that you may be able to bear it." 1 Corinthians 10[:13]

78 Morpheus

Text
Do not be too joyful or too worried
About the very distressing prophetic visions
Of Morpheus, who is messenger
Of the god who sleeps and makes dreams.

Gloss
Morpheus, so says a fable, is son of the sleeping god and his messenger; and is the god of dreams and makes dreams. And because the dream is a thing very troubled and obscure, and sometimes may signify the reverse that has been dreamed, he is not so wise as the expositors who may properly speak of them, which indicates to the good knight he should not be either overjoyed or worried about such prophetic dreams, by which one may not show certain significance nor to what they should turn, and namely that one should not be pleased or troubled by the matters of fortune, which are transitory. Socrates declares: "You who are men, you should not be overjoyed or troubled because of any event."

Allegory
When it says that he should not be too pleased or too troubled by prophetic dreams, we shall say that the good spirit should not be too pleased or too troubled by the things which befall him, and that he should bear tribulations peacefully. St. Augustine declares on the Psalter: "Beautiful son," says he, "if you weep over harms that you feel, then you weep under the correction of your Father; if you weep over the tribulations which come to you, beware that this is not out of indignation or pride, for the adversity that God sends to you, it is medicine, not pain, it is chastisement, not damnation. Never reject the rod of your Father, unless you wish that he reject you from his heritage; and never think of pain that you have from suffering his flail, but consider what place you have in his testament." To this purpose says the sage: "Let be what[1] shall be brought upon thee: and in thy sorrow endure, and in thy humiliation keep patience." Ecclesiasticus 2[:4]

79 Ceyx and Alcyone

Text
If on the sea you wish to undertake,
And make, a perilous voyage,
Believe the counsel of Alcyone:
I will tell you the danger of Ceyx.

---

1   Christine in fact substitutes "Let be what" for Vulgate's "Take all that."

Gloss

Ceyx was a very prudent king and much loved by Alcyone, his wife. The king observed a devotion to journey on the sea in a very perilous passage. He took to the sea during a weather storm, but Alcyone, his wife, who loved him exceedingly with a great passion, attempted in great pain to dissuade him from this voyage, and with great cries and many a teardrop prayed him, but it might not be remedied by her, nor did he wish to allow her to go with him, and so that she tried to the very end; and at the departure she threw herself toward the ship. But the king Ceyx again comforted her and with force made her remain, for which she was very anguished and inconsolable, for she was in too great an anxiety, after which Aeolus, the god of winds, blew so hard, they tossed about upon the sea. Ceyx the king within a few short days perished in the sea, after which, when Alcyone knew of the adventure, she threw herself into the sea. And the fable says that the gods will have pity thereof and transform the bodies of the two lovers into two birds, to the extent that their great love will be a perpetual memory. Thus the birds again fly on the sea, which are named "halcyons,"[1] and their feathers are white; and when the seafarers see them come, then they are sure to have a storm. The correct exposition of this fable may be that two lovers loved together in a like manner in marriage, which the poet has compared to two birds who had such a situation and adventure. Thus it means that the good knight should not put himself on a perilous voyage against the counsel of his good friends. And Assaron declares: "The wise man endeavors to avert injury, and the fool takes pain to find it."

Allegory

That in Alcyone you should believe, that is, that the good spirit is through evil temptation hindered by some error or doubt in his thought, for which he should report himself to the opinion of the Church. And St. Ambrose declares in the second book of *The Offices* that he is mad who despises the counsel of the Church, for Joseph helped the king Pharaoh more profitably with counsel of his prudence than if he had given him gold or silver, for silver was not provided for the famine of the realm of Egypt as was the counsel of Joseph, who remedied the famine of Egypt in the space of seven years. And after he concluded: "Believe counsel and you will never repent." To this purpose declares the sage in Proverbs in the person of the Church: "Keep the law and counsel: And there shall be life to thy soul." Proverbs 3[:21-2]

---

1 A type of kingfisher.

80 Troilus

Text
Do not agree with the counsel of a child,
And remember Troilus.
Believe the old and the expert,
And in charges of arms the skilled men.

Gloss
When the king Priam had finished reconstructing Troy, which because of the grieving of those who went to Colchos had been destroyed, then for that destruction Priam wished to take vengeance. Then he assembled his council, in which there were many exalted barons and sages, to know whether there would be good when Paris, his son, journeyed to Greece to ravish Helen in exchange for Hesione, his sister, who had been taken by Ajax Telamonius and placed in servitude. But all the sages agreed no, because of the prophecies and writings which said that because of this ravishment Troy would be destroyed. Then Troilus, who was a child and the youngest of the children of Priam, said that one should not believe, in the council of war, the old and the priests who counseled rest out of cowardice. So he counseled that one should not go there.[1] The advice of Troilus was taken, after which great evil ensued. For this indicates to the good knight that he should not hold to or believe in the counsel of a child, which naturally is of lighter and smaller consideration. To this purpose an authority declares: "The land is cursed where the prince is a child."

Allegory
To the counsel of a child the good spirit should not concede, which is to understand that he should not be ignorant but knowing and learned in that which may be profitable to his health. And against these ignorants St. Augustine states: "Ignorance is a very evil mother who has very evil daughters, which is to understand, falsity and doubt; the first is mischance; the second is miserable; the first is vicious, but the second is more annoying; and these two are removed by wisdom." About this the sage declares: "For regarding not wisdom, they did not only slip in this, that they were ignorant of good things, but they left also unto men a memorial of their folly." Wisdom 10[:8]

81 Calchas

Text
Hate Calchas and his accomplices,
Whose infinite malices

---

1 But wrong as he is, to be consistent with his earlier position he surely means that one *should* go there.

Betray realms and empires;
There exists in the world not another people worse.

Gloss

Calchas was a subtle clerk of the city of Troy; and when the king Priam knew that the Greeks were coming on him with a great host, he sent Calchas to Delphos to know from the god Apollo how he would fare in the war. But after the response of the god, who said that after ten years the Greeks would have the victory, Calchas turned toward the Greeks and acquainted himself with Achilles, who in Delphos had come for this same cause, and with him went toward the Greeks, the which he helped to counsel against his own city; and many a time afterwards disturbed the peace made between Greeks and Trojans. And because he was a traitor, indicates to the good knight that he should hate such subtle and evil people, for their reasons, made through deceit, may greatly damage realms and empires and all peoples. Therefore Plato declares: "The subtle enemy, poor and not powerful, may grieve more than the rich, powerful and not knowing."

Allegory

By Calchas, who should be hated, may be understood that the good spirit should hate all fraudulent malice against his neighbor, and should not consent to it. And St. Jerome says that the traitor does not soften either for familiarity of company, or for the matter of drink and meat, or for grace of service, or for an abundance of favors. Of this vice St. Paul the Apostle declares, "Men shall be ... covetous, haughty, proud, ... traitors, stubborn, puffed up." 2 Timothy 3[:2,4]

82 Hermaphroditus

Text

Do not be hard in conceding
That which you may well employ.
Consider Hermaphroditus,
Who received harm for refusing.

Gloss

Hermaphroditus was a young man of very great beauty. A nymph was much taken by love of him, but in no way would he deign to love her, and she pursued him through everything. And one time it happened that the gentleman was very weary from the hunt in which he had labored all day. Then he arrived at the fountain of Salmacis, where there was a beautiful pond, clear and tranquil, in which a desire to bathe seized him. He stripped off his clothes, and into the water he dove. When the nymph saw him wholly naked, she undressed and jumped after him and with great passion attempted to embrace the young man; but he, who was full of perfidy, tried to push her away with great rudeness, nor could she soften his heart for any [prayer]. Then the nymph, full of woe, prayed to the gods out of great desire that her lover, who rejected her so, might never part from her. The gods heard in pity her devout prayer, then suddenly transformed the two bodies into a single one which had two sexes. This fable may be understood in many manners, and like the clerks, subtle philosophers have hidden their great secrets under cover of fable, by which may be understood signification appertaining to the science of astronomy, and of necromancy as well, so as the masters say. And because the matter of love is more delectable to hear than any other, their fictions were commonly about love affairs in order to be more delightful, especially to the rude, who take nothing except the peel, and the more agreeable, to the subtle, who suck the liquor.[1] But in our discourse we may understand that it is an ugly thing and villainy to refuse, or to concede with great reluctance[2] that which may not turn to prejudice or to vice, being granted. And Hermes says: "Make no long delay to put into execution that which you should do."

Allegory

The good spirit should not be hard to grant there where it sees necessity, but to cheer up the needy in his power. As St. Gregory in the *Morals* declares, when we wish to cheer up someone afflicted with sadness, we should first sorrow with them, for he who does not agree with his woe may not properly cheer up the woeful. For, just as the one may not join one iron to another if both the two are not hot and softened by fire, so also we may not reform another if our heart is not softened by compassion. To this purpose Holy Scripture says: "Strengthen ye the feeble hands, and confirm the weak knees." Isaiah 35[:3]

83 Ulysses

Text

You may well amuse yourself in the games
Of Ulysses, in time and in place,
During truce and celebration,
For they are both subtle and honest.

Gloss

Ulysses was a baron of Greece of great subtlety; and in the time of long siege with Troy, which lasted ten years, when there were truces, he found subtle and very beautiful games to so entertain the knights when they were at rest. And some say that he invented the game of chess and

---

1 This image of hard shell and inner nut, rind and liquor, was frequently used to describe the false, outer layer of fiction (e.g., the classical myth) and the sweet, inner truth.

2 *Danger*, literally "danger," usually referred to the lady's disdain, which protected her in courtly love.

others like it. Therefore it is said to the knight that in due time he may well frolic in such games. And Solon says: "Every subtle and honest thing is fair to do."

Allegory

The games of Ulysses may be understood as, when the chivalrous spirit will be tired of praying and of being in contemplation, he may well entertain himself in reading Holy Scripture. For as St. Jerome declares in his *Morals*: "Holy Scripture is offered in the eyes of our heart as a mirror, to the extent that we may see in it the whole face of our soul. We may see there our beautiful [face], we may see there our ugly [face], we may see there how we profit and how we are far from profit." To this purpose says our Lord in the Gospel: "Search the scriptures, for you think in them to have life everlasting." John 5[:39]

84 Briseis (Criseyde)

Text

If you wish to give your heart
To Cupid and abandon everything,
Guard against acquainting yourself with Briseis,
For she had too roving a heart.

Gloss

Briseis was a gentlewoman of very great beauty, but also was very gracious, flighty, and seductive. Troilus, the youngest of the sons of Priam, was very full of great prowess, of beauty and of gentleness, the soul of great love, and she had given to him her love and had every day promised without falsifying. Calchas, father of the gentlewoman, who through science knew that Troy would be destroyed, did so much that his daughter was given up to him and taken outside the city and conducted to the camp of the Greeks, where he was. Great was the dolor of the two lovers at the departure, and their laments very piteous. Nevertheless, after a brief time, Diomedes, who was an important baron of the Greeks and a very valiant knight, acquainted himself with Briseis and worked so hard in his pursuit that she loved him and forgot entirely her loyal lover Troilus. And because Briseis had such a fickle disposition, it is said to the good knight that if he wishes to give his heart, that he guard against acquainting himself with a lady similar to Briseis. And Hermes says: "Guard yourself against the company of the evil, that you do not become one of them."

Allegory

Briseis, with whom he should beware of acquainting himself, is vainglory that the good spirit should in no way embrace, but flee with all his power, for it is too facile a thing and comes too suddenly. And St. Augustine on the Psalter says that he who has learned well and tried through experience to surmount the vices, is come to the recognition that the sin of vainglory, either entirely alone or most especially, is in perfect men to be avoided, for it is, among the sins, that which is the hardest to vanquish. Therefore St. Paul the Apostle says: "He that glorieth, may glory in the Lord." [1] Corinthians [1:31]

85 Patroclus and Achilles

Text

When you will have killed Patroclus,[1]
Then you should beware of Achilles.
If you do believe me, for it is all one,
Then goods between the two of them are communal.

Gloss

Patroclus and Achilles were companions together and such great friends that two brothers never loved each other more; and they and their goods were as a single thing. And because Hector killed Patroclus in battle came the great hate of Achilles for Hector, and from then on he swore openly his death. But because he doubted his [Hector's] great strength too much, never afterwards did he cease watching how he might surprise him uncovered and betray him. Thus Othea says to Hector, by prophecy of that which is to come, that, when he will have slain Patroclus, it will be necessary for him to beware of Achilles. And it is to understand that every man who has killed or mistreated a loyal companion of another, that the companion will attempt vengeance against him if he may. Therefore Madarge declares: "In whatever place that you may be with your enemy, hold him suspect every day, though it may be that you are stronger than he."

Allegory

That which he says, that when Patroclus will be slain, he should beware of Achilles, we may understand that, if the good spirit allows himself to incline to the enemy in sin, he ought to mistrust everlasting death. And as Solon says: "The present life is only a military expedition, and in sign of that this present life is called martial, in differentiation from that above, which is called triumphant, for it always has victory over enemies." To this purpose St. Paul the Apostle declares: "Put you on the armour of God, that you may be able to stand against the deceits of the devil." Ephesians 6[:11]

86 Echo[2]

Text

Watch that you do not reject Echo,
Nor despise her piteous complaints;

---

1   As indeed Hector will do: Othea has foreknowledge.
2   See also Fable 16, on Narcissus.

If you can endure her desire,
You do not know what is to come to you.

Gloss

Echo, so says a fable, was a nymph, and because, often being too much a great chatterbox, and in her chatter one day having denounced Juno, who watched her husband out of jealousy, the goddess was indignant about it, and said: "From now on you will speak no more first, but after another." Echo was amorous toward the beautiful Narcissus, but, for neither prayer nor sign of friendship she might make to him did he deign to have pity on her, and so much that the beauty died from love for him. But in dying she prayed to the gods that she might be avenged on him in whom she had found so much cruelty, that yet they might make him feel amorous sharpness, whereby he might experience the great sadness which courtly lovers,[1] who have been refused by lovers, have, and then it was necessary for her to die. Thus Echo expired, but the voice of her remained, which lasts still; and the gods made it everlasting in memory of this adventure, and it responds to people in these valleys and on the river after the voice of another, but it may not speak first. Echo may signify a person who through great necessity summons another. The voice which is delayed means that, of the needy people, there is enough remaining; and they may not speak except after another, means that they may not aid themselves without help from another. Therefore it is said to the good knight that he should have pity for the needy who require it. And Zaqualquin declares: "Who wishes well to guard the law should aid his friend with his goods, and preach to the sufferers— to be gracious, not to forbid justice to his enemy, and to guard himself against all vices and against dishonor."

Allegory

Echo, who should not be rejected, may be noted as mercy, which the good spirit should have in himself. And St. Augustine says, in the book on *The Sermon of our Lord on the Mount*, that those are blessed who willingly succor the poor, who exist in misery, for they deserve that the mercy of God deliver them from their miseries; and it is a just thing that, whoever wishes to be aided by a sovereign more powerful, so also he may aid the man inferior to him, inasmuch as he is more powerful than he. Therefore the sage says in his Proverbs: "He that is inclined to mercy shall be blessed." Proverbs 22[:9]

87 Daphne

Text

If you wish to have the laurel
Crown, which is better than other possessions,

---

1 *Les fins amans.*

It is necessary for you to pursue Daphne,
And you will have her by pursuing well.

Gloss

The fable says that Daphne was a gentlewoman whom Phoebus loved
as a beloved, and pursued her greatly, but she did not wish to be accorded
with him. One day it happened that he saw the beauty go on a path, and
when she saw him coming, she tried to flee, and the god after. And when
he was so close that she saw well that she might not escape, she made a
prayer to the goddess Diana[1] that she wished to save her virginity. Then
the body of the maiden was changed into a green laurel. And when
Phoebus approached, he took some of the branches from the tree and made
a wreath in sign of victory. And afterwards then from that, the wreath of
laurel signifies victory; and namely in the time of the great felicity of the
Romans, the victorious were crowned with laurel. The fable may have
many meanings, and it might happen that a powerful man pursued with
long travail a lady, and so much that under a laurel he attained his desire,
and for that cause from henceforth he loved the laurel and bore it on his
heraldic design, in sign of victory that he had of his love under the laurel.
And the laurel may also be taken as gold, which signifies nobility. And
because laurel signifies honor, it says to the good knight that he must
pursue Daphne, if he wishes to have a crown of laurel, that is to understand, pain and travail, if he would come to honor. To this purpose declares
Homer the poet: "By means of great diligence one comes to honor and
perfection."

Allegory

That it is necessary to pursue Daphne to have a crown of laurel, we
may understand that, if the good spirit wishes to have glorious victory, he
must have perseverance, which will lead him to the victory of Paradise,
of which the joys are infinite. As St. Gregory declares: "Where is," says
he, "the tongue which may suffice to relate it, and where is the understanding which can understand how many are the joys in that sovereign
city of paradise, to be always present among the orders of angels, with the
blessed spirits, to assist in the glory of the conductor, to behold the present
visage of God, to see the indescribable light, to be sure of never having
fear of death, to be joyful in the gift of everlasting immortality." To this
purpose David says in his Psalter: "Glorious things are said of thee, O city
of God." Psalms [86:3]

88 Andromache

Text

To you also I make mention
Of the prophetic dream of Andromache;

---

1 Her father Peneus in Ovid's *Metamorphoses* and the *Ovide moralisé* 1.3016-20.

> Do not dispraise your wife in everything
> Or other women well taught.

Gloss

Andromache was wife of Hector; and the night before he was killed, there came to the lady in a prophetic dream that the day that Hector would go into battle, without fail he would be slain. For which Andromache, with many a great sigh and tear, used her power so that he not go into battle, but Hector would not believe her, and there he was slain. Therefore, that the good knight should not entirely dispraise the prophetic dreams of his wife, that is to understand, the counsel and advice of his wife, if she is wise and well conditioned, and especially of other wise women. And Plato declares: "You should not dispraise your counsel from a little wise person, for though it be that you are old, do not be ashamed to learn, even if a child should show you, for on occasion the ignorant may advise the sage."

Allegory

The prophetic dream of Andromache, which should not be dispraised, means that the good purpose sent by the Holy Spirit should not throw away as nothing the chivalrous Jesus Christ,[1] but quickly put him into effect according to his power. From which St. Gregory says in his *Morals* that the good spirit, in order to attract us to doing well, admonishes us, moves us, teaches us; it admonishes our memory, it moves our will, and informs our understanding; the spirit, sweet and soft, does not suffer whatever little piece of straw to dwell in the habitation[2] of the heart wherein he inspires, but burns it up suddenly with the fire of his subtle circumspection. Therefore St. Paul the Apostle says: "Extinguish not the spirit." [1 Thessalonians 5:19]

89 Nimrod

Text

> If you have a great or busy war,
> Do not trust in the strength
> Of Babylon, for by Ninus[3]
> It was taken; rely on none of them there.

Gloss

Babylon the great was founded by Nimrod the giant, and it was the strongest city ever made; but notwithstanding it was taken by the king Ninus. Therefore it is said to the good knight that he should not trust so

---

1 Christ the Word as an Epiphany, or manifestation, of God is on another level like a prophetic dream believed by the ancients to be sent by the gods.

2 Straw was used to cover up (and warm) stone (and earth) floors. It was easily swept away and replaced when dirty.

3 "Minos" in other manuscripts.

much in the strength of the city or castle in time of war, for it may not be wholly furnished with people and with all that is necessary for suitable defense. And Plato says: "Whoever trusts only in his strength is often overcome."

Allegory

But the strength of Babylon in which one should not trust, it means that the good spirit should not rely on or await a thing that the world promises. And of this St. Augustine declares, in the book of *The Singularity of Clerics*, that it is too foolish a trust to account his life secure against the perils of the world; and a foolish hope it is to imagine being safe among the stings of sin, for little certain is the victory as long as one is among the lances of the enemies; and whoever is enveloped by flames is not easily delivered without burning. Believe in him who has the experience; even if the world laughs at you, do not have faith in it; let your hope be set in God. Therefore David says: "It is good to trust in the Lord, rather than to trust in princes." [Psalms 117:8]

90 Hector

Text

Hector, it is necessary to announce your death,
For which great heartfelt sorrow kills me.
That will occur when you do not believe
The king Priam, who will go with you praying.

Gloss

The day that Hector was slain in battle, Andromache his wife came to beg the king Priam, with very great complaints and weepings, that he should not allow Hector that day to go into battle, for without doubt he would be killed if he went there. Mars, the god of battle, and Minerva, goddess of arms, who in sleep had appeared to her, had certainly announced that to her. Priam tried as hard as he could that he not fight that day, but Hector stole away from his father and started out of the city by an underground passage and went to the battle, where he was slain. And because he had never disobeyed his father before this day, may be said that the day that he would disobey his father, then he would die. And it may be understood that no one should disobey his sovereign in reason, or his good friends, when they are wise men. And therefore Aristotle says to Alexander: "As long as you believe the counsel of those who use wisdom and who love you loyally, you will reign gloriously."

Allegory

Where she said to Hector that it is necessary to announce his death, that means that the good spirit should hold in continual memory the hour of death. Of this St. Bernard declares that one may never find of things human, a more certain than death, nor less certain than the hour of death;

for death has no mercy on poverty, nor bears the honor of riches; it does not spare wisdom, nor conditions, nor age; of death one does not have any other certainty except that it appears at the doors of the aged and in the clusters of the young. To this purpose says the sage: "Remember that death will not be slow."[1] Ecclesiasticus 14[:12]

91 Hector's Arms

Text
Again I intend to make you wise,
So that you have no habit in battle
To expose yourself out of your arms,
For then your death will open.

Gloss
Hector in battle was found discovered out of his arms, and then he was slain. And therefore it is said that he should not be discovered out of his arms in battle. And Hermes says: "Death is also like the stroke of an arrow and life is also like the arrow which is set to shoot."

Allegory
That which it says, that he should keep covered his arms, it is to understand that the good spirit should keep his sense closed, and never open. Of this St. Gregory declares that the person who leaves his judgment is similar to the juggler who finds no worse dwelling than his own; therefore he is everyday outside his dwelling, just as the man who does not keep his sense shut in is always rambling outside of the house of his conscience; and also he is the open hall where one may enter from every side. Therefore our Lord says in the Gospel: "having shut the door, pray to thy Father in secret." Matthew 6[:6]

92 Polyboetes

Text
Of Polyboetes do not covet
Arms; they are cursed.
For after the despoiling followed
Your death, through him who followed you.

Gloss
Polyboetes was a very powerful king, whom Hector had killed in battle after many other great deeds that he had done that day. And because he was greatly armed with beautiful and rich arms, Hector coveted them and bent down over the neck of his horse to despoil the body. And then Achilles, who had followed after him all in will to take him uncovered, wounded him below through the fault of the armor and with one blow sent him death, of which there was great injury, for a more valiant knight never

---

1 The Vulgate has "is not slow."

buckled a sword of which the stories make mention. And that such covetousness may be harmful in such a place, appears said through this case. Therefore the philosopher says: "Disordered covetousness leads man to death."

Allegory

That of Polyboetes one does not covet arms, we may note that the good spirit should not have covetousness of whatever worldly thing. For when it leads man to death, Innocent says in the book on the filth of the human condition[1] that covetousness is a fire which no one may eradicate, for the covetous man is never content to have that which he desires; for, when he has that which he desires, he desires more every day. Always he establishes his end in that which he tends to have and not that which he has. Avarice and covetousness are two extortioners who never cease to say: "Bring, bring!" And to the extent that silver increases, the love of silver increases. Covetousness is the way to spiritual death and many a time to corporal death. Therefore St. Paul the Apostle declares: "For the desire of money is the root of all evils." 1 Timothy 6[:10]

93 Achilles and Polyxena

Text
Do not besot yourself with foreign love;
Think of and understand the deed of Achilles,
Who foolishly thought to make
Of his enemy his beloved.

Gloss
Achilles was besotted with the love of Polyxena, the beautiful maiden, who was sister of Hector, and when Achilles saw her at the anniversary of the beginning of the year at the funeral for Hector in the time of truce, when many Greeks went to Troy to see the nobility of the city and of the rich obsequies for Hector, that were made the most solemn that had ever been made for the body of a knight. There Achilles saw Polyxena, where he was so taken by love of her that he might in no way survive. And therefore he sent to the queen Hecuba that he wished to contract marriage; and he would make the war cease and the siege depart, and would always be their friend. A long time Achilles was without his armor against the Trojans because of that love, and sent great pain to make the host depart, that which he could not do; and therefore the marriage was not made. And after that Troilus killed Achilles, who was entirely full of valor so that he was well the equal of Hector, his brother, in accord with the young age that he had. But about that the queen Hecuba was so wholly sad that she commanded him [Achilles] that he come to her in Troy in order to treat of the marriage. So he went there and was killed. Therefore it is said to

---

1 *De contemptu mundi* (*On Contempt for the World*), 2.6 (*PL* 217:719-20).

the good knight that with foreign love he should not besot himself, for through distant love many an injury is come. And therefore a sage declares: "When your enemies may not avenge themselves, then you have need to watch yourself."

Allegory

With strange love the good spirit should not besot himself, it is to understand that he should not love anything which is not entirely coming from God and terminated in him. Everything foreign, that is, the world, he should flee. And that he should hate the world, St. Augustine says in expounding the Epistle of St. John: "The world passes, and its concupiscence. O, then, reasonable man, which do you love more: either to love the temporal world and pass with time, or to love Jesus Christ and live perpetually with him?" To this purpose St. John says in his first Epistle: "Love not the world, nor the things which are in the world." 1 John 2[:15]

94 Ajax

Text

Never undertake arms foolishly;
It is peril, for body and for arms,
To take a naked arm and without shield.
Learn at least this through Ajax.

Gloss

Ajax was a very proud and overweening Greek knight, but a good knight he was in his hand. And through pride and gallantry undertook arms with his arm naked and discovered without his shield, so he was pierced through and through and overthrown dead. Therefore it is said to the good knight that performings of such arms are not from any honor, also are reputed foolish and proud, and are too perilous. And Aristotle says about this: "Many err through ignorance and fault of knowing, and do not know whether to do it or leave it; and others fail through arrogance and pride."

Allegory

How arms should not be undertaken foolishly, means that the good spirit should not trust in his own fragility. As St. Augustine declares in a *Sermon* that no one should presume in his heart when he pronounces a word, nor should anyone trust in his strength when he suffers temptation, for when we speak good words wisely, it comes from God, not from our wisdom; and when we endure adversities steadfastly, it comes from God, not from our patience. To this purpose says St. Paul: "And such confidence we have, through Christ, towards God. Not that we are sufficient to think any thing of ourselves,
as of ourselves." 2 Corinthians 3[:4-5]

95 Antenor

Text

Exile and chase away Antenor,
Who against his country purchased
Treason, falsity, and disloyalty;
Thus, giving him up would be harmful.

Gloss

Antenor was a baron of Troy; and when it came to the end of the great Trojan battle, the Greeks, who had held the long siege in front of the city, did not know how to bring to a head taking the city, for it was of great strength. Then, by the instigation of Antenor, through the anger that he had toward the king Priam, he comforted them and said that they should make a peace with the king, and through his path would put themselves in the city and passage would be given them. Thus it was done, through which Troy was betrayed. And because that treason was too great and evil, it is said to the good knight that all those similar to him, where he knows them, he should chase away and exile, for such people evoke too much hatred. Plato says: "Deceit is the captain and governor of the wicked."

Allegory

By Antenor, who should be chased away, we may understand that the good spirit should chase away from himself everything through which disadvantage might come to him. About this St. Augustine declares that he who is not too preoccupied to avoid the disadvantages is like a moth, who flutters so much around the fire of the lamp that his wings burn and that after, he is drowned in the oil; and to the bird, who flies so much around the glue-covered twig[1] that he loses his feathers. The example of St. Peter, who dwelled so long in the court of the prince of the law that he succumbed to such a disadvantage of abjuring his master. For this the sage declares: "Flee from it, pass not by it." Proverbs 4[:15]

96 Minerva's Temple

Text

In the temple of Minerva you should not
Suffer your enemies to make offerings.
Beware of the horse of wood;
Troy would still be, if it had not existed.

Gloss

The Greeks had made peace through a fantasy with the Trojans by means of the treason of Antenor. They said that they had dedicated a gift to Minerva the goddess which they wished to offer; and they had created a horse of wood of marvelous grandeur, which was full of armed knights;

---

1 Used to catch birds.

and it was so great that it was necessary to break the door of the city for it to enter. And the horse was set on wheels which rolled it up to the temple; and when night had come, then the knights leapt out, those who were set outside in the city, who killed all the people and destroyed the city. For this says to the good knight that he ought not to trust in such fantasies nor in such offerings. To this purpose says a wise man: "One should doubt the subtleties and the traps of his enemy, if he is wise; and if he is foolish, his unpleasantness."

Allegory
By the temple of Minerva we may understand Holy Church, in which nothing should have been offered except prayer. St. Augustine says in the book *On Faith* that, without the fellowship of Holy Church and baptism, one may not profit at all, nor may the works of pity be of use, nor everlasting life, nor outside the lap of the Church may be healthy. For this David says in the Psalter: "With thee is my praise in a great church." [Psalms 21:26]

97 Ilium

Text
Do not think to have sure possessions,
For Ilium, the strong castle,
Was taken and burned, as was Tunis.
All is within the hands of Fortune.

Gloss
Ilium was the master dungeon of Troy, and the strongest and most beautiful castle that ever was made of which histories make mention; but notwithstanding it was taken and burned and came to nothing, and so was the city of Tunis, which at one time was a great thing. And because such cases happen through the mutability of Fortune would indicate that the good knight should not be proud or hold himself certain because of any strength. For this Ptolomy says: "By so much as a lord is raised higher, by so much is the downfall more perilous."

Allegory
That he does not think to have sure possessions, we may understand that the good spirit should not have regard or regret for any manner of delights. For as delights are passable, not certain, and leading to damnation, St. Jerome says that it is impossible that a person pass from delights to delights, and that she leap from delights of this world to the delights of paradise, which fill the belly here and the soul there. For the divine condition is so apportioned it is never given to those who think to have the world everlasting in delights. To this purpose it is written in the Apocalypse: "As much as she hath glorified herself, and lived in

delicacies, so much torment and sorrow give ye to her." Apocalypse 18[:7]

98 Circe

Text
You should avoid the port of Circe,
Where the knights of Ulysses
Were changed into pigs.
Remind yourself of her methods.

Gloss
Circe was a queen who had her kingdom on the sea of Italy, and was a very great enchantress and knew much of sorcery and witchcraft.[1] And when Ulysses, who traveled by sea after the destruction of Troy, and so thought to return to his country after many a great torment and perils which he had, had arrived at the port of the same land. He asked the queen through his knights if he might securely take haven in her country. Circe received these knights most fairly and through a semblance of courtesy tried to tender them a very delicious beverage to drink, but the potion had such strength that suddenly the knights were transformed into swine. Circe may be understood in various manners. And it may be understood as a land or a country where the knights were put in foul and villainous prison. And she may be also a lady full of idleness, and that through her several errant knights, that is to understand, following arms, which namely were of Ulysses' people, that is to understand, malicious and crafty, were kept to sojourn as swine. And therefore it is said to the good knight that he should not remain in such a sojourn. And Aristotle says: "He who is wholly inclined to fornication may not at the end be praised."

Allegory
The port of Circe we may understand as hypocrisy, that the good spirit should avoid in all things. And St. Gregory speaks against hypocrites in his *Morals*, that the life of hypocrites does not exist unless as a fantastic vision and an imaginary fantasy, which shows on the outside a likeness of an image, the which is not inwardly real in truth. To this purpose says our Lord in the Gospel: "Woe to you ... hypocrites, who[2] are like to whited sepulchres, which outwardly appear to men beautiful, but within are full of dead man's bones, and of all filthiness." Matthew 23[:27]

---

1 "Mioultemens," a word not identified by Loukopoulos, is translated "witchcraft" by Scrope.
2 "Because you" appears instead of "who" in the Vulgate.

99 Ino

Text
You should not tender beautiful explanations
To him who is not able to understand them.
Ino, who sowed corn suddenly,
Signifies it to you sufficiently, as I indicated.[1]

Gloss
Ino was a queen who tried to sow corn quickly, which did not come up. And therefore it is said to the good knight that beautiful reasons well ordered and wise authorities ought not to be told to people of rude understanding and whoever cannot understand them, for they will be lost. And therefore Aristotle says: "Just as rain does not help corn sown on stone, no more do arguments help the ignorant."

Allegory
[This fable means] that beautiful words should not be said to the rude or to the unknowing, who will not understand them, as this will be a thing lost, but instead [the good spirit] should blame the appearance of ignorance. St. Bernard declares in his book *The Fifteen Degrees of Humility* that for naught are those who, to the extent that they sin most freely, excuse themselves because of frailty or ignorance, are willingly frail and ignorant, and many things which ought to be known are on each occasion unknown, either through negligence in understanding them, or through slowness in asking about them, or through shame in searching for them. And all such ignorance has no excuse. Therefore St. Paul the Apostle says, "But if any man know not, he shall not be known." 1 Corinthians 14[:38]

100 Caesar Augustus and the Sibyl

Text
One hundred authorities I have written to you;
If they are not despised by you,
For Augustus learned from a woman,
Who taught him about being worshiped.

Gloss
Caesar Augustus was emperor of the Romans and all the world; and because, in the time of his reign, peace existed through all the world, so that he reigned peaceably, the foolish people believed that they held that peace which existed because of the good from him; but that was not so, for it came about through Jesus Christ, who was born of the Virgin Mary and lived during that time on earth; and while he was there, peace prevailed through all the world. So they wished to worship Caesar as God.

---

1 Above, in Fable 17.

But then the Cumaean Sibyl said to him to guard well that he not make himself to be worshiped, and that there was no god but one, who had created everything. And then she led him to a high mountain outside the city, and in the sun, through the desire of our Lord, appeared a Virgin holding an Infant. The Sibyl showed it to him and said to him that this was the true God, who ought to be worshiped; and therefore Caesar worshiped him. And because Caesar Augustus, who was prince of all the world, learned to know God and belief from a woman, to this purpose may be said the authority which Hermes stated: "Do not be ashamed to hear truth and good teaching, whoever may say it; for truth ennobles whoever pronounces it."

Allegory

There where Othea says that she has written to him one hundred authorities and that Augustus learned from a woman, is to understand that good words and good teaching bring praise to whichever persons have said them. From which Hugh of St. Victor says this—in a book named *Didascalicon*—that the wise man listens willingly to everything and learns willingly from each, and reads willingly all kinds of teaching; he does not despise Scripture; he does not despise the individual; he does not despise the doctrine; he searches dispassionately through everything, and all that he sees, for that which he has lacked; he does not consider who it is who speaks, but what it is that he says; he does not take heed to watch how he himself knows, but how much he does not know. To this purpose says the wise man: "A good ear will hear wisdom with all desire." Ecclesiasticus 3[:31][1]

---

1 The last word in Christine's text is in fact *sapiencia*, "wisdom."

Interpretative Essay

Christine's Minerva, the Mother Valorized

Certainly even her critics agree that Christine promoted the education of women; defended their virtue and wisdom by resurrecting examples of wise, virtuous, and saintly women in *City of Ladies* (1404-5); and late in her life celebrated Joan of Arc's heroic victory at Orléans and the coronation of Charles VII in one of her last works, *Le Ditié sur Jehanne d'Arc* (*The Tale of Joan of Arc*) (1429). Her interest in the Amazons and in Pallas Athena and Minerva, and her friendships with famous and powerful aristocratic women like Marie de Berry and Isabeau of Bavaria remind us of how sympathetic she was to strong women, how modern-seeming she was. Indeed, her literary construction of the Gothic castle in the *City of Ladies* (by means of the help of contemporary, classical, and early medieval women) is brought to life when, in her last years, because of the threat of civil war, she retreats to the convent of Poissy. There her daughter had for some time served as a nun—in a veritable "city of ladies" whose defensive virtues might well consist of reason, justice, and righteousness.

But how much of a feminist was Christine? And how dangerous is it to read her work from a modern, and therefore anachronistic, feminist perspective? Susan Schibanoff, in "Taking the Gold out of Egypt: The Art of Reading as a Woman," notes that "In the *Othea*, Christine schooled herself in the art of reading as a man or, more accurately, a patristic exegete....Perhaps because of its very traditional and patriarchal re-readings, the *Othea* was extraordinarily successful" (pp. 91, 92). Because of her patristic orientation, we might infer that Christine shares little or nothing with contemporary feminist theorists who advocate the rewriting of history, and of tradition to reflect female concerns and modes of perception and being.

In line with such an inference, in the *City of Ladies*, Christine indeed subscribes to the idea that Reason governs emotions in both men and women, and at the end, she advises the wives of bad husbands to endure their brutality and to help to ameliorate their characters. Chastity, again and again, is seen as an ideal for women. She identifies her own role as poet as important in the Dantesque, aristocratic, and masculine sense expressed in *De monarchia* (*On Monarchy*): the poet has an obligation to improve society and counsel those imperial rulers in their divinely-sanctioned role as head of state. For example, *L'Avision-Christine* (*Christine's Vision*) (1405), a kind of autobiography dealing with many subjects—philosophy, religion, history, cosmology, etc.—as an allegorical vision also portrays Christine as a scribe for La Dame Couronne, or France, with

Charles V once again depicted as the just monarch in his *noblesse de courage* (nobility of courage), *chevalerie* (chivalry), and *sagesse* (wisdom). Perhaps, as Sheila Delaney scoffs in a recent essay, "'Mothers to Think Back Through': Who are They? The Ambiguous Example of Christine de Pizan," Christine is the Phyllis Schafly of the Middle Ages in her "rearguard" social thought and ultra-conservative political views, at a time Delaney defines as rebellious and liberal for women of various classes.

Yet I think this view deeply underestimates the subtle power of her feminism and her ability as a thinker and writer. If Christine can be supposed to agree with Geoffrey La Tour Landry (p. 122) that parents should teach their daughters how to read so that the wives of bad husbands will help change their faults by recognizing dangers to the soul—a course of action she seems to explicitly encourage at the end of the *City of Ladies* and implicitly throughout the *Othea*—then Christine's own rereadings of women in both works are polemical. Indeed, in the former work, when Christine asks Reason about the intellectual ability of women, she discovers women are not only by nature equally as intelligent as men but are, in fact, probably more intelligent, given the harmonious balance that characterizes the chain of being which structures the created world:

> I tell you again—and don't doubt the contrary—if it were customary to send daughters to school like sons, and if they were then taught the natural sciences, they would learn as thoroughly and understand the subtleties of all the arts and sciences as well as sons. And by chance there happen to be such women, for, as I touched on before, just as women have more delicate bodies than men, weaker and less able to perform many tasks, so do they have minds that are freer and sharper whenever they apply themselves. (Richards, 1.27.1, p. 63.)

Reading—the goal of the first three arts of medieval education, the *trivium* (grammar, rhetoric, dialectic) for Christine becomes a feminist activity, a subversive act of revision of the tradition, the text, of woman. It is no accident that the personifications of Reason, Justice, and Righteousness respond to Christine's despair in *City of Ladies*: the allegorical equivalents of Pallas-Minerva, Penthesilea, or Diana, Ceres, and Isis, they will remind Christine of aspects of human ability characteristic of women—instead of reasoning powers, then ingenuity, instead of strength, then courage, instead of an inclination to lechery, then chastity, virtue, and religious faith. One must read Christine carefully, understand how subtly she rereads and alters the mythographic tradition, in order to see how subversive a reader she was.

Many contemporary French and American feminist theorists have used mythological figures—Medusa, Pandora, and Echo, among others—

to convey their ideas concerning women's language, sensibility, writing. Women, they say, differ from men: if western culture has promoted the intellectual, phallocentric approach to life, then it should now begin to speak the language of the body, of the subconscious—of Echo. Or, to use another myth, men, paralyzed by Medusa, have always identified women with the body rather than with intellectual powers, but then they have ignored the body and privileged the intellect from the earliest periods. In reaction, Helene Cixous focuses on the "laugh of the Medusa" with which women should respond to this damaging situation. Because men have riveted women between Medusa and the Abyss, afraid to look straight at the Gorgon, who represents two unrepresentable things (death and the female sex), because Perseus turned away from the Medusa, women must respond by writing the body. Only then can the Medusa laugh. By writing the body Cixous means using the language of female sexuality, of woman's anger and her joy. The ink with which women must write is "white milk" (p. 59). Women's bodies, especially when they occupy the role of mothers, become that "dark continent," in Cixous's words, that needs to be explored. In particular, "Woman must give woman to the other woman" (p. 60)—as a maker of children, she will give herself to her "child."

If one agrees with Cixous that women are different but not inferior, their difference being a result of their biology, then are there signs of this difference in Christine? Does the mythographer emphasize the quotidian realism of everyday life, to appeal to the more sensuous and sensual nature of women? Do we see the blood, milk, and tears so familiar to women from parturition, lactation, and weeping? Has the new affective spirituality of the thirteenth century conditioned her response to the mothers she reconstructs for us? Does she see Jesus as mother, nurturing and supportive (or is this paradigm a reflection only of modern perspectives of the role of the mother)?

Indeed, Christine feminizes the mythographic tradition, valorizing the female, although perhaps not in the exact way heralded by Cixous. She refocuses attention away from the negative (*in malo*) view of woman's sexual role as man's playmate, to her positive (*in bono*) parturitional and lactational role as mother of children, creator and educator. The power of woman, because of her ingenuity, or creativity, and faith, resides in her ability to make things grow—especially, and more morally, the virtues, whether in herself or others. She is also a *virago* and fighter able to use her virtue and understanding to protect herself. Accordingly, Reason in *City of Ladies* asserts the concept of balance in Nature—Reason says, "if Nature did not give great strength of limb to women's bodies, she has made up for it by placing there that most virtuous inclination to love one's God and to fear sinning against His commandments. Women who act otherwise go against their own nature" (Richards 1.14.2, p. 37).

An example of how Christine rereads the tradition and rewrites woman, using the language of the body, becomes apparent from her use of the myth of Minerva, or Pallas Athena. It is she who aids the hero Perseus in overcoming the same figure used as a paradigm by Cixous— Medusa. For Christine, Minerva is a prototype for all women—the mother of Hector, self-created, wise and valorous, a self-sufficient and resourceful armor-maker who can defend herself against attack. She also fulfills the ideal role for woman, as the prudent mother who educates her children and nourishes their virtues in order to protect them from assault. This is in contrast to Medusa, who was ravished by Phoebus (rather than Neptune, according to Christine) in Diana's temple and whose subsequent anger over her victimization "mothers" only the stone into which she transforms all men (it is no accident that in the traditional mythographies Medusa signifies oblivion). The two images, of lactational nourishment and of armor-making, or the city as armor, recur throughout the *Letter of Othea*, but as we shall see, are always set against the stone or serpent (barren, dead, dangerous) imagery associated with Medusa.

Minerva, as inventor of armor, becomes a mother in the sense of author and protector (13). The knight will have assigned to him a new mother, because of his need for armor:

> Armors of all kinds
> With which to arm, well-made and strong,
> By your mother will be delivered to you,
> Minerva, who is not bitter to you.

So Othea calls Hector "son of Minerva," as all who love arms may be named. Christine reforms the role to emphasize matrilineal connections instead of patrilineal ones. In the "Allegory" for this text (13), Christine explains this good armor as faith (as in Ephesians 6), "which is a theological virtue and is *mother* to the good spirit" (my italics). This feminization of the maker of armor is continued in the description of faith, seen as a gate of paradise or window of life, ground of health—a door, or entry way, like the cervix through which the child enters life: "And that she delivers enough armors, Cassiodorus says in the *Exposition on the Creed* that faith is the light of the soul, the door of paradise, the window of life, and the foundation of everlasting health."

Christine celebrates the generative body of the mother figure, understood both literally and allegorically. Guidance and direction reproduce— engender—bring to birth—"children," in this case the virtues. Note in the first fable, of Othea, that the mythographer explains that "prudence and wisdom are *mother* and conductress of all virtues, without which the others could not be well governed," and because it is necessary for the good knight to be "adorned with prudence," the knight must be educated with this "array" of examples to amend "contrary things" (p. 38, my italics), according to St. Augustine, whom Christine quotes frequently.

Othea, then, as prudence and wisdom in particular, will "mother" the virtues in "virtuous chivalry." The text will accordingly instruct the youth as a mother instructs her son, as Christine in fact was instructing her own fifteen-year-old son. For this reason her most powerful figures in the *Letter* are mothers, female warriors, and female scholars.

Minerva represents the mother (of Hector, of the soul) because she has mothered herself, leaping self-created and fully-formed out of Jupiter's head, unlike Eve, whom God formed out of Adam's rib, although both Eve and Pallas appropriate the birthing process for the male. For Christine, Minerva signifies the goal of male birth—to mother the prudence and virtue the goddess intends for Hector's self-education.

The earliest mythographers interpreted Minerva's self-birth from Jupiter's head as a particularly male quality—the strength of intellectual endeavor, and virility of mind. As early as the sixth-century mythographer Fulgentius, Minerva is also offered as an example of virility and manhood in his allegorization of the story of Aeneas in Virgil's epic journey:

> So I began with "arms," knowing that the noun "man" is a designation of sex, not of praiseworthiness: for if I put the noun "man" first, there are many men, but not all of them praiseworthy. Therefore, I placed manliness first, as the quality for which I assumed man should be praised, following Homer who says "The wrath do thou sing, O goddess, of Peleus's son, Achilles," indicating the man's anger before the particular man. Then, too, when he shows manliness in the symbol of Minerva, he describes how she gripped fast Achilles' hair. (*Expositio*, #8, Whitbread, p. 123.)

"Manliness" is nevertheless controlled by the mind, through wisdom:

> As I started to say, manliness is the essential quality, but wisdom is what controls this essence, just as Sallust declared: "For all our strength lies in the mind and the body." (*Expositio*, #10, Whitbread, p. 124).

Most important, Fulgentius links her iconographic description with the Gorgon Medusa, whom she defeated through Perseus: the relationship morally connotes the mind's mastery over fear.

> They associate her with the Gorgon, worn on her breast as a symbol of fear, just as the wise man bears awe in his breast to guard against his enemies. They give her a plume and helmet, for the mind of the wise man is both armed and noble whence Plautus in his *Trinummus* declares: "It certainly has a head like a mushroom, it covers him completely." She is also enfolded in a robe of three folds, either because all wisdom is many-sided or because it is kept hidden. She also carries a long spear, because wisdom strikes at long range with its pronouncements. The dress has three folds also be-

cause all wisdom is concealed from without and is rarely seen. They also choose to put the owl in her charge, because wisdom has its flashes of lightning even in the dark. Whereby they also claim that she was the founder of Athens, and Minerva in Greek is called Athene, for *athanate parthene*, that is, immortal virgin, because wisdom cannot die or be seduced. (*Mythologies*, Whitbread, p. 65)

This same interpretation in the hands of the fourteenth century English mythographer Robert Holkot, commenting on the book of Wisdom, will be Christianized, with Pallas's wisdom born from God and the peace she brings by means of miseries the peace of God; her threefold dress by which she is covered up and decorated represent the three literary arts of the *trivium*—from which, we will remember, Christine as a woman was barred from learning in the medieval schools.

At first glance, Christine, by means of the figure of Pallas Athena/Minerva, seems to be reacting against the misogyny of her countryman Boccaccio, who had declaimed against the strong woman, the *virago*, as unnatural. In his *De claris mulieribus* (*Concerning Famous Women*) (1355-59), he declares in writing of his famous women, "What can we think except that it was an error of nature to give female sex to a body which had been endowed by God with a magnificent virile spirit?" (Guarino, p. 127). We are reminded that Christine, in the midst of mourning over the loss of her husband and brother and cheated out of her inheritance by unscrupulous lawyers, in order to function better in the world, wished to be transformed into a man, in both body and will, in the *Mutation of Fortune* (1400-3).

Of course, Christine clearly admires Minerva literally and understands the excellence of women as military leaders: indeed, the *Livre des trois vertus* (*Book of the Three Virtues*) (1405) asks women to learn the principles of command, defensively or offensively. Christine was much taken with chivalry, arms, and military virtues, including the Amazons and Joan of Arc. Note that "L'Epistre de la prison de vie humaine et d'avoir reconfort de mort d'amis et pacience en adversite," or "Letter Concerning the Prison of Human Life, and On Having Consolation upon the Death of Friends and Patience in Adversity" (1416-18) as a letter of consolation was inspired by those men who died at the Battle of Agincourt (1415) and is dedicated to Marie de Berry, Duchess of Bourbon (her friend), who also suffered personally because of this battle. Note also her treatise on the art of warfare (a synthesis of ancient and medieval sources), *Le Livre des fais d'armes et de chevalerie* (*Feats of Arms and Chivalry*) (1410), which influenced international law in its argument that war is lawful for a just cause, either self-defense, defense against tyranny, or preserving freedom of a country; she also discusses weaponry, military strategy, and laws of conflict. And in the later *City of Ladies*—a *Portrait of the Artist* to this

Stephen Hero—Christine will very clearly reveal, especially in the first book, the history of women military leaders, rulers, and queens—warmakers all.

However, Minerva also functions as Hector's mother, in Christine's novel casting of the maternal guide (in the most medieval and therefore unmodern way) as prudent rather than tender. For Christine, good mothering is good guidance or direction—education: in the Middle Ages, the mother, at least for women and young boys, was the chief educator. The relationship between son and mother here is loving, but the power of the mother, as inventor of that which will protect the son, derives again from her skill, her ingenuity, and her creativity. The son then reflects or images forth the power or strength of the mother as her product, her "work." It is therefore no accident that human communion with Christ, literally, through the experience of eating his Body in the form of the Eucharist, but more figuratively through imitation of God, is likened to the nursing of the child at the breast: in Fable 9, on Apollo, the god of truth often likened to Christ in the mythographies, Christine declares, "we may take that one ought to have in the mouth truth, the real knight Jesus Christ, and must flee all falsity."

The traditionally perceived emotionality of mothers, and their tears, undergo similar metamorphoses in Christine's text, as powerful catalysts for change. For this reason the so-called non-rationalism of the Trojans—their self-indulgence and venery—lends itself to Christine's purpose in feminizing the education of Hector and repudiating the false (masculine) cunning of the Greeks. Penthesilea (15), Queen of the Amazons, admires the valor of Hector and therefore becomes "despondent out of moderation" after his death. She then channels her depression outward by summoning a "host of gentlewomen" to avenge his death at the hands of the Greeks "very chivalrously." In a sense another mother for Hector, Penthesilea is so revealed by Christine's Allegory: "By Penthesilea, who gave succor, we may understand the virtue of charity." With this nurturing (read as "protective") mother Christine again images forth regenerative moisture, as charity (love) was also revealed in the fontenal symbolism of baptism: "Cassidorus says that charity is also like the rain which falls in spring, for it distills the drops of the virtues under the which grain good will and good deed fructify." Thus, the figure of the virtuous Penthesilea who should be loved by every good knight means both that the knight should love every virtuous person, "and similarly a woman strong in virtue of intelligence and constancy." Such a strong woman is also evident in the *City of Ladies* in the mother Berenice. Her maternal tears fuel her military efforts: after her former husband's brother had killed two of her sons in battle in an attempt to disown her sons, "she was so grieved that her anger purged her of all feminine fear" (1.25.1). Like Christine mourning the loss of her husband, father, and son, Berenice "took up arms herself and with a great army advanced against her brother-in-law and fought so hard that in the end she killed him with her own hands, had her chariot driven over him, and won the battle" (Richards, pp. 61-2).

Even more conventional interpretations are slightly reworded to reflect the power of the angry mother, greater than that of a tearful mother, especially if the tears are appropriately directed and channeled, as was Penthesilea's (15). Achilles, foolishly trusting the mother of the children he had so treacherously slain (40), namely Hector, tries to arrange a marriage with Hecuba's daughter Polyxena and is thereafter slain by Paris and his friends. The incessant tears of Aurora (44), spring of the day, over the loss of her son Tynus slain in the battle of Troy, compel her to transform her son into a swan—signifying that the good knight should *rejoice* in his virtues and should not succumb to depression and despair.

Even the divine Father is transformed into a divine "Mother," a trinity of classical goddesses—Diana as God the Father (23), Ceres as the Son Jesus Christ (24), Isis as the Holy Ghost (25). Their divine "mothering," or impregnation, results in the increase of virtues in the soul, metaphorically instanced in the conception of Christ within Mary. Such an increase occurs within the soul as the seed takes root inside the womb. Diana (23), literally the moon, was "named after a lady, called so," and, allegorically, because she remains chaste and virgin, signifies God in Heaven "without any spot of unclean love." Ceres (24), too, literally a "lady who invented the art of tilling the land, for before, they sowed the arable lands without a plough," is venerated as a goddess of corn after the people notice that "the land bore more abundantly after it had been tilled." But it is her understanding of generation which the people celebrate—she understands how the earth may better bear fruit. In this sense, the good knight should emulate her because Ceres, like the second person of the Trinity, Christ, has given to us so "liberally" of "high goods." Finally, Isis (25), as goddess "of plants and of cultivating," is a model mother: she "gives them strength and increase to multiply." That is, she reminds the good knight to fructify in all virtues and avoid vices in an image again rooted in the conception of Jesus Christ by the Holy Ghost within the womb of the Virgin Mary, "mother of all grace." The act of conception is masculine, but the good spirit is feminine and plays the role, in this trope, of the Virgin. In relation to the act, Christine notes, "the which worthy Conception the good spirit ought to have wholly in himself, and hold firmly the worthy article, as says St. James the Greater: 'Who is conceived by the Holy Ghost, is born of the Virgin Mary.'"

The figure of the mother is most important for Christine, finally, not because of her ability to bear children or express maternal feelings openly by means of her tears, but because of her lactational ability and what that signifies morally. The most dramatic example may be that of Io (29), who in the mythographies is glossed as a type of carnality because Jove consorted with her and then transformed her into a heifer to protect her from Juno's jealous wrath. For Christine, euhemerizing once again, "the poets have hidden truth under cover of fable." In her fable, Io is a young gentlewoman who is loved by Jupiter for her virtues and thus said to become a cow because the letters (alphabet) she strikes out with her hoof to communicate are intellectually nourishing, like the cow's milk. Christine declares, "it can be understood that Jupiter loved her, that is to mean, the virtues of Jupiter which existed in her. She became a cow, for just as the cow gives milk, which is sweet and nourishing, she gave, through the letters which she invented, sweet nourishment to the understanding." On the allegorical level, the alphabet invented by Io becomes the Holy Writ and Scriptures that allow the good spirit to climb to heaven through good works and contemplation. Again, faith is feminine and begins with prudence, mothering the virtues. Note also that Christine revises the charge that Io was a prostitute: if she is a common woman then she is common in the sense that her wit is common to all, "as letters are common to all people."

Christine similarly and radically reinterprets the legends of other classical women, often to demonstrate their learning or their roles as educating and virtuous models, especially in the role of mothers. Cassandra (32) is treated as "a very good lady and devout in their law." Speaking little without cause, she does not lie and she "honored the temple," as the good knight, who is also a good Christian, should. Likewise, Pyramus and Thisbe (38) are reminders that we should worship father and mother, against whom these children rebelled by falling in love.

Curiously, Medusa (55), the adversary of Minerva and her hero Perseus in the classical myth, in Christine's fable also comes to represent the opposite of tears and "engendering laughter"—that is, the opposite of that mothering (restraining, controlling, developing) and engendering (enlarging, broadening) associated here with both Minerva and Perseus (5). The good spirit, a model for the female reader, then identifies not with Medusa but with Minerva and the ideal hero she helpfully instructs in arming himself against the Gorgon. It is Perseus whom Christine counsels to avoid worldly delights: "compunction is the *mother* of tears and pleasures *engender* laughter" (my italics); or, according to Psalms 125:5, "They that sow in tears shall reap in joy." Christine puts the idea yet another way, "compunction *restrains* the heart and pleasure *enlarges* it" (my italics).

For Christine, however, as for Cixous, Gorgon (Medusa) in 55 is initially not so much sinning as sinned against. The only late medieval mythographer who recaptures this ancient and more positive view of the figure, Christine sees Medusa as a beautiful noblewoman with whom Phoebus (rather than Neptune) lies in the temple of Diana, thereby offending the goddess so grievously that she transforms her into a serpent that can turn men to stone. It may be that Medusa's unintended violation of the Temple of Diana—an invasion of the temple sacred to the goddess of chastity—is being used here to contrast with the Temple of Minerva at the end (Fable 96), a type of Holy Church. That is, Christine adds to the Ovidian fable the idea that the Gorgon represents a town transformed into a (curiously phallic and therefore male) serpent because of its many vices (harming neighbors, robbing them, etc,); Perseus protects himself from the evil city by looking at his reflected strength and knighthood in his shield. By this change Christine means that her text, like the shield reflecting the image of his strength and knighthood, will mother her female reader—in this encyclopedia the reader will see, and thereby strengthen, her self as reflected in these examples of strong, wise, virtuous women. The problem, so Christine reminds us, is that Medusa was never a mother.

A mother, very like a fortified town, protects her charges as Minerva the mother will protect Hector (and Perseus). Christine juxtaposes and contrasts various women as images of good or bad towns or castles in her *Letter*, particularly the two we have been discussing—Gorgon as a bad town, and Minerva as a good one. She includes especially Circe (98), a great enchantress who is understood as a land where Ulysses's knights are imprisoned foully (that is, transformed into swine after drinking a potion), or a wanton and idle lady on whose behalf many knights avoid arms. Allegorically the swine (like the frogs and the serpent above) represent hypocrisy which the good spirit should avoid, the image of their life, unlike the image in Perseus's shield, understood, according to St. Gregory, as a "fantastic vision and an imaginary fantasy."

The image of the city was used by other medieval poets to define the security and safety of the eternal home of man, with God. Such images include the heavenly Jerusalem, in Augustine's *City of God*; the apocalyptic vision at the end of *Pearl*; the barn of Unity (or the Church) in which Piers Plowman and his followers shelter from the Antichrist in William Langland's poem of the same name; and of course antithetically the hellish City of Dis in Dante's *Inferno* in which the fallen angels as frogs guard the gate.

Other, more troubled cities loom large in Christine's mythological treatises, whether in the *City of Ladies* or the *Letter*—types of the City of Man, or of Cain, divided by the discord and sin of *cupiditas*. The city of Thebes, founded by Cadmus, falls to the Greeks—Theseus of Athens— eventually. Its origin in the serpent's teeth which spring up as armed soldiers after Cadmus sows them remind us that it is a city divided from within. The city of Troy, founded by Laomedon, also falls to the Greeks led by Ulysses. Its walls, built with Neptune's help, are built through an act of treachery in that Laomedon reneges on his promise to pay the god, and the treachery of the first, and founding king of the city is echoed in the treachery involved in its fall through Priam's brother Antenor. Equally strangely, when Christine returns to Minerva at the end of the *Letter* in her text on Minerva's temple (96), her temple becomes Holy Church, to which prayer should be offered as a gift rather than the Trojan horse filled with murderous and deceitful Greeks: the good knight should not trust in "such fantasies nor in such offerings."

For Christine, the metaphor of the city in the *City of Ladies* will be used to structure the tripartite work: Reason will lay the foundation, Justice will provide the walls, and Righteousness will add the towers and pinnacles. Intended to provide community for women, like a convent, and to protect them against the natural and moral threats from the outside world, the city of women functions like the kingdom of the soul in John Gower's *Confessio Amantis*. These "reflections in Perseus's shield" are collected into three books differentiated from each other through an emphasis on virtue, although in all three Christine minimizes their relationships with men. In Book One, we see three sections, on military skill and strategy (pp. 30-62), or ladies of political and military deeds; arts and sciences— poets, inventors, sorcerers, painters (ladies of learning and skill, pp. 27-42); clothmakers, housewives, city-founders (ladies of prudence, pp. 43-8). In Book Two, the women are chaste and morally right; in Book Three, Justice, they are saintly and holy martyrs, chaste and faithful, their intelligence and mind overcoming the tortures of the body.

Throughout the *Letter* Christine will consistently euhemerize female figures similar to these archetypal ones. That is, she will not reread the text offered by female figures in the same way as the male mythographers have before her—for she often feminizes the misogynistic tradition of mythography in her fresh readings—but instead to reveal new aspects of these "mothers" of prudence and virtue, just as she frequently associates male figures with sin and ignorance.

However, if the mother as source is understood through the gynecological image of the womb—the fountain, the well—and of mois-ture—the rain-drops, the vein—then the biology of maternality can also be used negatively, *in malo*, as it was in the conventional misogynist mythographies to convey viciousness—Eve's error. Vices can also be "mothered." The example used by Christine occurs in the figurative "mothering" of Venus, in fable 7, who generates evils and is associated with concupiscence by means of the female image of the fountain. Christine declares, "Vanity is *mother* of all evils, the fountain of all vices and the vein of iniquity" (my italics).

Bad mothers, like Queen Ino (17), stepmother to Athamas's children, are evil precisely because they cut off or disinherit their children: instead of guiding or protecting them, they destroy them and their family, and therefore weaken the society from which they come. Ino exiles her two stepchildren because the corn she had sown makes no profit (or else she bribes the priests of the law to say so). For this reason, Juno, goddess of childbirth and the archetypal cosmic mother, complains in hell to the "goddess of madness" to afflict Athamas, in an act of vengeance normally interpreted by the mythographers as revenge for Jupiter's act of dalliance with Semele, the daughter of Cadmus, who founded Thebes. Thereafter, mad Athamas kills both his children and also Ino. The bad mother, then, is bad in her malice and in her disinheriting of her children, which causes dissension between husband and wife and death and madness for all—the destruction of the family. The ire of Athamas, Christine explains in an Augustinian and quotidian image used in her allegory, is like vinegar that lies too long in a barrel and "corrodes" its vessel. Once again, a womb image is associated with moisture and destruction rather than construction.

Often Christine will use female sexual symbols to identify the vice of a city, which she associates, however, with the male. In the fable of Latona (20), pregnant with Apollo and Diana and chased by Juno from country to country, when she is chided by churls at the water where she thirstily drinks, she curses them to live ever after as frogs in the "swamp" (20). Christine identifies the common "swamp" as the sin of avarice, that is, such communities of men who are displeasing to masters should be cast into the river and drowned. Once again, the good knight should not "sully himself in the swamp of villainy." Similarly, a quotidian wine image pejoratively types the "feminine" god Bacchus (21), son of Semele who was nurtured in Jove's thigh after his mother's violent and fiery death. Naturally he is associated with the planting of vines (in Greece first), but more tropologically, with drunkenness, and, according to Hippocras, the superfluity of wines and meats which destroys the body.

To interpret woman negatively, *in malo*, in the misogynistic mythographic tradition, is to portray her as suffering from excessive carnal appetites, although Christine turns even this interpretation to her own spiritual purpose. That is, she often uses what appear to be evil female figures to represent errant knights, or types of the soul who should be gently redirected to God. If Pasiphae depicts dissolution, allegorically she represents a fool, or a soul returned to God (45). Coronis (48), despite the raven's accusation of adultery, is not in fact revealed as adulterous: Apollo regrets murdering her and seems to be mistaken in accepting the raven's (false?) counsel. In the Allegory, Christine remarks that Coronis should not be slain (by sin) because she represents our soul. Citing St. Augustine, Christine adds, "the soul ought to be kept as a chest which is full of treasure, as the castle which is besieged by enemies, and the king who rests in his room of retreat." The use of the womblike container and room image serves to recollect the female associations of the body—but never wholly pejoratively. Rehabilitation is always possible. Medea (58), "one of the most knowing women of sorcery," who nevertheless allowed herself to be mastered by "fole amour" (wanton love) for Jason, giving him her devotion through her body and her goods. From this Othea warns the good knight in the Gloss not to allow his reason to be overcome by delight in pleasure, and in the allegory the good spirit not to allow the will to have domination. Likewise, Semele (62), who, in the hands of the mythographers, is a brazen and fornicating woman, becomes a loving woman deceived by Juno into asking Jupiter to appear to her in the same form as he does his wife—the fable of her curiosity transformed into a lesson on the "science of astronomy," or a warning that a gentlewoman can be deceived by the wife of her love and therefore die inadvertently—so that a good knight should be wary of revealing secrets. Similarly, the lust of Salmacis for Hermaphroditus (82), when she saw him undressed, relates to "signification appertaining to the science of astronomy, and of necromancy as well."

In the final fable (100), as in the *Metamorphoses*, Augustus is introduced, but as the disciple of a wise Pallas-like woman: "For Augustus learned from a woman/ Who taught him about being worshiped." We learn that although the time he reigned was peaceful, it was not because of his goodness but because of Jesus Christ, "who was born of the Virgin Mary" at the same time. Although the people wished to worship Augustus as a god, the Sibyl instructed him that there was only one God and led him to a mountain outside town where he had a vision of the Lord as a child in the arms of the Virgin. Allegorically, Augustus learning from a woman, says Christine, means that good words and good teachings mirror the person saying them: "good words and good teaching bring praise to whichever persons have said them," whether pagan or Christian, male or female. Othea's hundred fables, lessons for Hector, all center on the acquisition of wisdom—the last word of text in the book, *sapiencia*—but more importantly, wisdom written by a woman. Sibyl in the last fable addresses, or converts, Augustus, just as Othea, throughout, addresses, or educates, Hector, and just as Minerva mothers, or protects, Hector. On all these levels it is in reality Christine who addresses, converts, educates, mothers, and subverts her reader.

Appendix A:

A Medieval Genealogy of the Gods
(From the First Vatican Mythographer, Myth 204)

I. The Major Gods and The Royal Hero of Troy: Aeneas

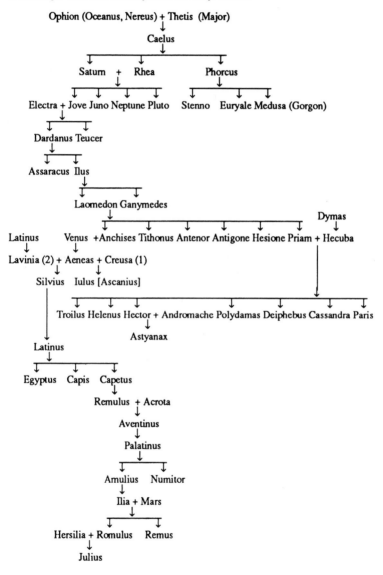

Ophion (Oceanus, Nereus) + Thetis (Major)
↓
Caelus
↓

Saturn + Rhea   Phorcus
↓
Electra + Jove Juno Neptune Pluto   Stenno Euryale Medusa (Gorgon)
↓
Dardanus Teucer
↓
Assaracus Ilus
↓
Laomedon Ganymedes
↓   Dymas
↓
Latinus   Venus +Anchises Tithonus Antenor Antigone Hesione Priam + Hecuba
↓   ↓
Lavinia (2) + Aeneas + Creusa (1)
↓   ↓
Silvius   Iulus [Ascanius]

Troilus Helenus Hector + Andromache Polydamas Deiphebus Cassandra Paris
↓
Astyanax
Latinus
↓
Egyptus Capis Capetus
↓
Remulus + Acrota
↓
Aventinus
↓
Palatinus
↓
Amulius Numitor
↓
Ilia + Mars
↓
Hersilia + Romulus Remus
↓
Julius

II. The Royal Kings of Greece

A. The House of Atreus

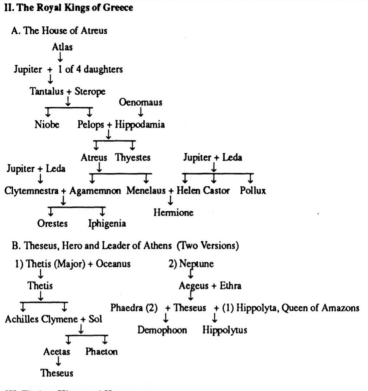

```
                    Atlas
                      ↓
        Jupiter + 1 of 4 daughters
                  ↓
            Tantalus + Sterope
                  ↓          Oenomaus
          ┌───────┴───┐         ↓
        Niobe    Pelops + Hippodamia
                        ↓
                  ┌─────┴─────┐
              Atreus  Thyestes        Jupiter + Leda
  Jupiter + Leda  ↓                  ↓
        ↓     ┌───┴────┐        ┌────┴────┬────┐
  Clytemnestra + Agamemnon  Menelaus + Helen  Castor  Pollux
        ↓                           ↓
    ┌───┴───┐                   Hermione
  Orestes  Iphigenia
```

B. Theseus, Hero and Leader of Athens (Two Versions)

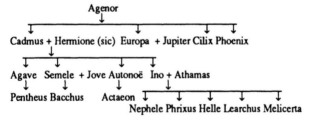

```
  1) Thetis (Major) + Oceanus        2) Neptune
              ↓                           ↓
           Thetis                     Aegeus + Ethra
              ↓                           ↓
      ┌───────┴──┐        Phaedra (2) + Theseus + (1) Hippolyta, Queen of Amazons
  Achilles  Clymene + Sol             ↓          ↓
                  ↓              Demophoon   Hippolytus
            ┌─────┴─────┐
          Aeetas    Phaeton
            ↓
          Theseus
```

III. Theban Kings and Heroes

A. Cadmus, Founder of Thebes, and Brother of Europa

```
                    Agenor
                      ↓
  ┌───────────┬──────┴───────┬──────────┬──────┐
  Cadmus + Hermione (sic)  Europa + Jupiter  Cilix  Phoenix
      ↓
  ┌────┬───────┬─────────┬──────┐
  Agave  Semele + Jove  Autonoë  Ino + Athamas
    ↓        ↓            ↓        ↓
  Pentheus Bacchus    Actaeon  ┌───┬──────┬─────┬────────┬────────┐
                            Nephele Phrixus Helle Learchus Melicerta
```

B. Amphion, Theban Hero and King (after Cadmus and brother Zethus)

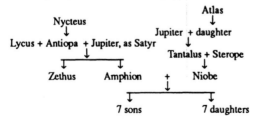

```
                                      Atlas
            Nycteus                     ↓
              ↓             Jupiter + daughter
  Lycus + Antiopa + Jupiter, as Satyr      ↓
              ↓                  Tantalus + Sterope
      ┌───────┴───┐                      ↓
    Zethus     Amphion      +       Niobe
                      ↓
              ┌───────┴───────┐
            7 sons         7 daughters
```

C. King Oedipus and his Sons and Daughters-in-Law

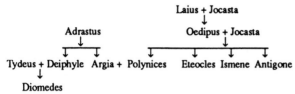

```
                              Laius + Jocasta
                                    ↓
            Adrastus               Oedipus + Jocasta
               ↓
        ┌──────┴──────┐      ┌──────┬───────┬───────┐
   Tydeus + Deiphyle  Argia + Polynices  Eteocles Ismene Antigone
       ↓
    Diomedes
```

D. Meleager and his sister Deianira (wife of hero Hercules)

```
        Mars
         ↓            Thestius
      Parthaon           ↓
         ↓        ┌───────┼───────┐
      Oeneus + Althea  Toxeus Plexippus
         ↓                         Jupiter + Alcmena + Amphitryon
    ┌─────┬──────┬─────┐                   ↓
 Meleager Gorge Tydeus Deianira  +    Hercules
                                  ↓
                                Hylas
```

IV. The Genealogy of the Secondary Gods

A. Apollo   B. Mercury   C. Jupiter's semen or Juno's thigh
                                                          ↓   ↓
            Coeus   Jupiter + Maja   Vulcan   Vulcan
              ↓   ↓
        ┌─────┴─────┐   Mercury
  Jupiter + Latona Titanus + Terra
        ↓   ↓
   ┌────┴────┐   12 sons against the gods
  Apollo   Diana

D. Jupiter's head   E. Juno + Jupiter   F. Saturn (testicles, cut off by Jupiter)
       ↓   ↓   ↓
  Pallas (Minerva)   Hebe   Venus

G. Jupiter (as golden shower) + Danaë   H. Jupiter (as swan) + Leda + Tyndarus
                 ↓   ┌───────┬───────┐
              Perseus   Egg 1   Egg 2   Egg 3
                                          (Castor + Pollux) (Clytemnestra) (Helen)

V. Children of Secondary Gods and Genealogies of Wives of other Minor Kings

A.   Lycurgus   B.   Aeeta + Hypsea
                 ↓   ↓
          ┌──────┴──────┐   ┌───────┬───────┐
Demophoon + Phyllis Archemorus Calciope Medea + Jason Absyrtus

C. Admetus + Alceste   D.
         ↓   Phlegias + Ixion
    ┌────┴────┐   ↓
  Nisa Stenobea + Proteus   Apollo + Coronis
                                             ↓
                                       Aesculapius

E. Apollo + Ethea   F. Apollo
        ↓   ↓
      Circe   Pasiphaë + Minos
```
```

G.

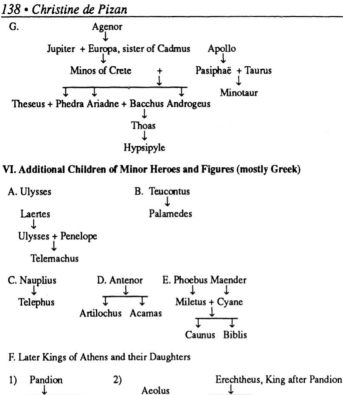

```
                        Agenor
                          ↓
        Jupiter + Europa, sister of Cadmus      Apollo
                     ↓                            ↓
              Minos of Crete      +        Pasiphaë + Taurus
        ┌──────┬──────────┬──────┐    ↓              ↓
                                              Minotaur
   Theseus + Phedra Ariadne + Bacchus Androgeus
                          ↓
                        Thoas
                          ↓
                      Hypsipyle
```

VI. Additional Children of Minor Heroes and Figures (mostly Greek)

```
A. Ulysses                    B. Teucontus
                                     ↓
   Laertes                     Palamedes
      ↓
   Ulysses + Penelope
         ↓
    Telemachus
```

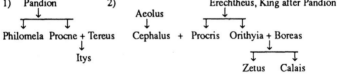

```
C. Nauplius        D. Antenor      E. Phoebus  Maender
      ↓                 ↓              ↓         ↓
   Telephus      ┌──────┴──────┐    Miletus + Cyane
              Artilochus  Acamas        ↓
                                  ┌─────┴─────┐
                               Caunus     Biblis
```

F. Later Kings of Athens and their Daughters

```
1)    Pandion         2)                Erechtheus, King after Pandion
         ↓                   Aeolus              ↓
   ┌─────┴─────┐               ↓          ┌──────┴──────┐
 Philomela  Procne + Tereus  Cephalus + Procris  Orithyia + Boreas
                ↓                                      ↓
              Itys                            ┌────────┴────────┐
                                            Zetus           Calais
```

Appendix B: A Chronological List of Major Medieval Mythographers
4th-7th centuries

Servius (ca. 389), Commentaries on Virgil's *Eclogues, Georgics*, and *Aeneid*

Macrobius (ca. 433), *Saturnalia*; Commentary on the *Somnium Scipionis*

Fulgentius (fl. 468-533), *Mitologiae; Expositio Continentiae Virgilii; Super Thebaiden*

Isidore (fl. 602-636), *Origines* (8.11.1-104, "De diis gentium")

8th-11th centuries

First Vatican Mythographer (8th-10th c.?), Mythography

Theodulf of Orleans (ca. 786), "De libris quos legere solebam et qualiter fabulae poetarum a philosophus mystice pertractentur"

Hrabanus Maurus (776?-856), "De diis gentium" of Isidore copied in *De universo*

Second Vatican Mythographer (9th-10th c.?), Mythography

Remigius of Auxerre (ca. 841-908), Commentaries on Martianus Capella and Boethius

Ecloga Theoduli (9th c.)

Notker Labeo (d. 1022), Commentaries on Martianus and Boethius

Bernard of Utrecht (11th c.), Commentary on *Ecloga Theoduli*

Baudri of Bourgueil (1046-1130), Poem CCXVI: Fragment of a Moralized Mythology

12th-13th centuries

William of Conches (1090-1145), Commentaries on Boethius, Macrobius, Martianus Capella, Juvenal, the *Timaeus*

Bernardus Silvestris (1085-1178), Commentaries on the *Aeneid* and Martianus Capella

Third Vatican Mythographer (12th c.), *De diis gentium et illorum allegoriis*

Arnulf of Orleans (fl. 1175), Glosses on Lucan, Ovid's *Metamorphoses*, and Ovid's *Fasti*

John of Garland (1180-1252), *Integumenta Ovidii*

14th-15th centuries

Nicholas Trevet (ca. 1314), Commentaries on Boethius, St. Augustine's *City of God*, Seneca's *Tragedies*

Ovide moralisé (14th c.)

John Ridevall (fl. 1331), *Fulgentius metaforalis*, Commentary on *City of God*, 1-3, 6-7

Giovanni del Virgilio (fl. 1332-3), *Allegorie librorum Ovidii Metamorphoseos*

Robert Holkot (fl. 1332-4, d. 1349?), Commentaries on the Book of Wisdom, the Twelve Prophets, Ecclesiastes

Pietro Alighieri (ca. 1340-1), Commentary on Dante

Pierre Bersuire (ca. 1342), *Ovidius moralizatus*

Giovanni Boccaccio (fl. 1313-75), *Genealogie gentilium deorum*, Commentary on the *Inferno*

Coluccio Salutati (1331-1406), *De laboribus Herculis*

Christine de Pizan (ca. 1399), *Epistre d'Othéa*

Cristoforo Landino (fl. 1481), Commentaries on Virgil and Dante

Appendix C: A Table of Sources for Mythological Figures in Christine de Pizan's *Letter of Othea*

Fable and Figure(s)	Source
1 Othea	*The Assembly of Gods*
1 Hector	no known source
3 Hercules	*Ovide moralisé* 7.1681-1951
4 Minos	*Ovide moralisé* 2.5074-80
5 Perseus	*Ovide moralisé* 4.6586sq and Ovid 4.610sq
6 Jupiter	*Ovide moralisé* 1.721-6
7 Venus	*Ovide moralisé* 1.727sq
8 Saturn	*Ovide moralisé* 1.640-3, 513-718, 7109-866
9 Apollo	no known source
10 Phoebe (The Moon)	no known source
11 Mars	no known source
12 Mercury	no known source
13 Minerva	no known source
14 Pallas and Minerva	no known source
15 Penthesilea 4.2135-84	no known source; see *Confessio Amantis*
16 Narcissus also Gower 1.2275sq	Ovid 3.341sq and *Ovide* 3.1854- 1902,
17 Athamas	*Ovide* 4.2804-2928 and 3834-3963
18 Aglauros	Ovid 2.737sq and *Ovide* 2.3777- 4076
19 Ulysses and Polyphemus	Boethius commentaries on 4m3
20 Latona	Ovid 6.313sq and *Ovide* 6.1581- 1772
21 Bacchus	*Ovide* 3.823-45 and 2528-76
22 Pygmalion	*Ovide* 10.929-1074
23 Diana (the Moon)	no known source
24 Ceres	no known source, touched on in *Ovide* 5.1846-9
25 Isis	Boccaccio's *De claris*
26 Midas	Ovid 11.146-93 and *Ovide* 11.651-770
27 Pirothous and Theseus	*Ovide* 7.1681-1951
28 Cadmus	*Ovide* 3.1sq and 4.5116sq (and others, including Chaucer's *Knight's Tale*, Bersuire, and Lydgate's *Siege of Thebes*
29 Io ancienne, plus *Ovide* 1.3450-4	Boccaccio's *De claris* ll. 902-3, and *Histoire*
30 Mercury and Argus	Ovid 1.3408-3796 and Bersuire
31 Pyrrhus	no known source
32 Cassandra	no known source; *Cité des dames*
33 Neptune	no one source
34 Atropos Siege of Thebes and The Assembly of Gods.	Statius's *Thebaid* 3.68, also Lydgate's
35 Bellerophon	*Ovide* 4.5892-995
36 Memnon	*Ovide* 12.4508
37 Laomedon	*Ovide* 7.196-242

38 Pyramus and Thisbe	details from *Ovide* 4.219-1169; the *Cité des*
dames 2.56	
39 Aesculapius and Circe	*Ovide* 2.2426-9 and 2993sq
40 The Death of Achilles	*Ovide* 12.4305-4579
41 Busiris	Boethius commentaries on 2p6
42 Leander and Hero	*Ovide* 4.3150-3586; Machaut's *Jugement dou roy*
de Navarre and *Cité des dames*	
43 Helen	no known source
44 Aurora	*Ovide* 12
45 Pasiphae	*Ovide* 8.617-986
46 Adrastus	*Ovide* 9.1537-1838, possibly also prose Ovide
(Bersuire), with the story cited in *Cité, Mutacion, Les Enseignemens*	
47 Cupid	various sources
48 Coronis	*Ovide* 2.2121-2622
49 Juno	*Ovide* 1.4110-11
50 Amphiaraus	*Ovide* 9.1622
51 Saturn the Saturnine	various sources
52 Apollo's Crow	*Ovide* 2.2160sq
53 Ganymedes	*Ovide* 10.787-817
54 Jason	*Ovide* 7.8646 and the *Histoire ancienne*
55 Gorgon	*Ovide* 4.5637-5713, 5714-5891
56 Mars and Venus	Ovide 4.1268-1371 and Lydgate's *Temple* ll.
126-8	
57 Thamaris	*Histoire ancienne*; *Mutacion* ll. 9535-9802 and
Cité	
58 Medea	*Cité*, *De claris* 1357-8 and Lydgate's *Troy*
Book 1.3694-5	
59 Galatea	*Ovide* 13.3689
60 Peleus	*Ovide* 11.1242sq (also the Prose Ovid)
61 The Death of Laomedon	*Ovide* 7.196-249
62 Semele	*Ovide* 3.701-810, from Ovid 3.253-315
63 Diana	*Ovide* 3.357-570 and Ovid 3.131- 252
64 Arachne	*Ovide* 6.1-318 and in *Cité*
65 Adonis	*Ovide* 10.1960-2093
66 The First Troy	*Ovide* 7.196-242 and 7.8646, as well as the
Histoire ancienne	
67 Orpheus	*Ovide* 10.708-17 and 11.1-10
68 Paris	*Ovide* 12
69 Actaeon	*Ovide* 3.357-570, or Ovid 3.131- 252 and
Gower 1.333	
70 Orpheus and Eurdice	Ovide 10.1-195
71 Achilles	*Ovide* 12.1101-63, also Holkot's *Convertimini*
and Gower's *Confessio* 5.2961	
72 Atalanta	*Ovide* 10.2094-2437
73 Judgment of Paris	*Ovide* 11.1830-2189 and the *Histoire*
74 Fortune	no one source
75 Paris the Warrior	no known source

76 Cephalus	*Ovide* 7.2759-3282, from Ovid 7.661-865
77 Helenus	no known source
78 Morpheus	no known source but in *Ovide* 11
79 Ceyx	*Ovide* 11.2996-3393 and also the Prose Ovid
80 Troilus	*Histoire ancienne*
81 Calchas	*Histoire ancienne* and Orosius and the *Ystoire de Troye*
82 Hermaphroditus	*Ovide* 4.1997-2223, or Ovid 4.285-388
83 Ulysses	no one source
84 Briseis	*Histoire ancienne*
85 Patroclus	*Ovide* 12.3514sq
86 Echo	*Ovide* 3.1292-1463
87 Daphne	*Ovide* 1.2737-3064, or Ovid 1.452-567
88 Andromache	*Histoire ancienne*
89 Nimrod	*Ovide* 1.2425sq and the *Histoire ancienne*
90 The Death of Hector	*Histoire ancienne*
91 Hector's Arms	*Histoire ancienne*
92 Polyboetes	*Histoire ancienne*
93 Achilles and Polyxena	*Histoire ancienne*
94 Ajax	no known source
95 Antenor	*Histoire ancienne*; Orosius and the *Ystoire de Troye*
96 Minerva's Temple	*Histoire ancienne*
97 Ilium	no known source
98 Circe	*Ovide* 14.2355-2562, also in *Mutacion* and *Cité des dames*
99 Ino	no known source
100 Caesar Augustus and Sibyl	*Legenda aurea*

N. B. This data was compiled in part from Curt Bühler's notes in his edition of *'The Epistle of Othea': Translated from the French Text of Christine de Pisan by Stephen Scrope* (London: EETS, 1970), based in part on P.G.C. Campbell, *L'Épître d'Othéa: Étude sur les sources de Christine de Pisan* (Paris: Champion, 1924), esp. Section II, pp. 63-184.

Suggestions for Further Reading

I. The Mythographic Tradition in the Middle Ages and Medieval Poetic

A. Primary Texts

Bernardus Silvestris. *Commentary on the First Six Books of Virgil's Aeneid.* Trans. Earl G. Schreiber and Thomas E. Maresca. Lincoln and London: University of Nebraska Press, 1979.

Bersuire, Pierre. "The *Ovidius Moralizatus* of Petrus Berchorius: An Introduction and Translation." Trans. William Reynolds. Dissertation University of Illinois, 1971.

Boccaccio, Giovanni. *Concerning Famous Women.* Trans. Guido A. Guarino. New Brunswick, N.J.: Rutgers University Press, 1963.

——————————. *On Poetry.* Trans. Charles G. Osgood, 1930. Rpt. Indianapolis: Bobbs-Merrill, 1956.

Bode, Georgius Henricus, ed., *Scriptures Rerum Mythicarum Latini Tres Romae Nuper Reperti.* 2 vols. 1834; rpt. Hildesheim: Georg Olms, 1968.

Boethius. *The Consolation of Philosophy.* Trans. Richard H. Green. Indianapolis and New York: Bobbs-Merrill, 1962.

Chaucer, Geoffrey. *The Riverside Chaucer.* Ed. Larry D. Benson. 3rd. ed. rev. from F. N. Robinson. Boston: Houghton Mifflin, 1987.

Dante. *The Divine Comedy.* Trans. John Sinclair. 3 vols. 1939; rpt. New York: Oxford University Press, 1981.

Fulgentius, Fabius Planciades. *Fulgentius the Mythographer.* Trans. Leslie George Whitbread. Columbus: Ohio State University Press, 1971.

Guillaume de Lorris and Jean de Meun. *The Romance of the Rose.* Trans. Charles Dahlberg. Princeton: Princeton University Press, 1971.

Macrobius. *Commentary on the Dream of Scipio.* Trans. William Harris Stahl. Records of Civilization: Sources and Studies, no. 48. 1952; rpt. New York and London: Columbia University Press, 1966.

Ovid. *Heroides.* Trans. Grant Showerman. Loeb Classical Library. 2nd ed. Cambridge, Mass.: Harvard University Press; London: William Heinemann, 1977.

Ovid. *Metamorphoses.* Ed. and trans. Frank Justus Miller. 2 vols. Loeb Classical Library. 3rd ed. Cambridge, Mass: Harvard University Press; London: William Heinemann Ltd., 1977.

B. Secondary Texts

Barkin, Leonard. *The Gods Made Flesh.* New Haven: Yale University Press, 1988.

Bloch, R. Howard. *Etymologies and Genealogies: A Literary Anthropology of the French Middle Ages.* Chicago: University of Chicago Press, 1983.

Chance, Jane. "From Homer to Dante: The Origins and Development of Medieval Mythography." In *Mapping the Cosmos.* Ed. Chance and R. O. Wells. Houston: Rice University Press, 1985. Pp. 35-64, 151-9.

Friedman, John Block. *Orpheus in the Middle Ages.* Cambridge: Harvard University Press, 1970.

Green, Richard H. "Classical Fable and English Poetry in the Fourteenth Century." *Critical Approaches to Medieval Literature.* Ed. Dorothy Bethurum. New York: Columbia University Press, 1960.

Hyde, Thomas. "Boccaccio: The Genealogies of Myth." *PMLA*, 100 (1985), 737-45.

Panofsky, Erwin. *Studies in Iconology: Humanistic Themes in the Art of the Renaissance.* New York: Oxford University Press, 1939.

Schreiber, Earl G. "Venus in the Medieval Mythographic Tradition." *JEGP*, 74 (1975), 519-35.

Seznec, Jean. *The Survival of the Pagan Gods: The Mythological Tradition and its Place in Renaissance Humanism and Art.* Trans. Barbara F. Sessions. Bollingen Series, vol. 38. New York: Pantheon Books, 1953.

II. Feminist Studies and Feminist Theory
A. Women in the Middle Ages

Baker, Derek, ed. *Medieval Women.* Oxford: Blackwell, 1978.

Bynum, Caroline Walker. *Holy Feast and Holy Fast.* Berkeley: University of California Press, 1986.

————————————. *Jesus as Mother.* Berkeley: University of California Press, 1982.

Chance, Jane. *Woman as Hero in Old English Literature.* Syracuse: Syracuse University Press, 1986.

Davis, Natalie Zemon. *Society and Culture in Early Modern France.* Palo Alto: Stanford University Press, 1975.

Diamond, Arlyn, and Edwards, Lee R., ed. *The Authority of Experience: Essays in Feminist Criticism.* Amherst: University of Massachusetts Press, 1977.

Dronke, Peter. *Women Writers of the Middle Ages.* Cambridge: Cambridge University Press, 1984.

Erler, Mary, and Maryanne Kowaleski, ed. *Women and Power in the Middle Ages.* Athens and London: University of Georgia Press, 1988.

Ferrante, Joan M. "The Education of Women in the Middle Ages in Theory, Fact, and Fantasy." In *Beyond their Sex: Learned Women of the European Past.* Ed. Patricia H. LaBalme. New York: New York University Press, 1980. Pp. 9-42.

————————————. *Woman as Image in Medieval Literature: Literature from the Twelfth century to Dante.* Durham, North Carolina: Labyrinth Press, 1985.

Lucas, Angela M. *Women in the Middle Ages: Religion, Marriage and Letters.* Brighton, Engl: Harvester Press, 1983.

Power, Eileen. *Medieval Women.* Ed. M. M. Postan. Cambridge: Cambridge University Press, 1975.

Rose, Mary Beth, ed. *Women in the Middle Ages and Renaissance: Literary Perspectives.* Syracuse: Syracuse University Press, 1986.

Shahar, Shulamith. *The Fourth Estate: A History of Women in the Middle Ages.* London and New York: Methuen, 1983.

Stuard, Susan Mosher. *Women in Medieval History and Historiography.* Philadelphia: University of Pennsylvania Press, 1987.

Warner, Marina. *Joan of Arc: The Image of Female Heroism.* New York: Alfred A. Knopf, 1981.

B. Feminist Theory

deBeauvoir, Simone. Introduction to *The Second Sex.* New York: Vintage, 1974. Rpt. in *New French Feminisms: An Anthology.* Ed. Elaine Marks and Isabelle de Courtivron. New York: Schocken Books, 1981.

Cixous, Helene. "The Laugh of the Medusa." In Elaine Marks and Isabelle de Courtivan. Eds. *New French Feminisms.* New York: Schocken, 1981. Pp. 245-264. French version in *L'Arc* (1975), 39-74.

Culler, Jonathan D. "Reading Like a Woman." In *On Deconstruction: Theory and Criticism after Structuralism.* Ithaca: Cornell University Press, 1982.

Daly, Mary. *Pure Lust: Elemental Feminist Philosophy.* Boston: Beacon Press, 1984.

Downing, Christine. *The Goddess.* New York: Crossroad Publishing, 1981.

Gilligan, Carol. *In a Different Voice.* Cambridge: Harvard University Press, 1982.

Greenberg, Caren. "Reading Reading: Echo's Abduction of Language." In *Women and Language in Literature and Society.* Ed. Ruth Borker, Nell Furman, Sally McConnell-Ginet. New York: Praeger, 1980.

Kristeva, Julia. "Hérethique de l'amour." *Tel Quel,* 74 (Winter, 1977), 30-49. Rpt. as "Stabat Mater." In *Histoires d'amour.* Paris: Denoël, 1983. Re-ed. slightly and trans. Arthur Goldhammer. *Poetics Today,* 6, 1-2 (1985), 133-52. Rpt. in *Histoires d'amour.* New York: Columbia University Press, forthcoming.

Miller, Nancy K., ed. *The Poetics of Gender.* New York: Columbia University Press, 1986.

Munich, Adrienne. "Notorious Signs, Feminist Criticism and Literary Tradition." In *Making a Difference: Feminist Literary Criticism.* Ed. Gayle Greene and Coppelia Kahn. London and New York: Methuen, 1985. Pp. 238-59.

Nye, Andrea. "Woman Clothed with the Sun: Julia Kristeva and the Escape From/To Language." *Signs,* 13 (1987), 664-86.

Ostriker, Alicia. "The Thieves of Language: Women Poets and Revisionist Mythmaking." *Signs*, 8 (1982), 68-90.

Schibanoff, Susan. "Taking the Gold out of Egypt: The Art of Reading as a Woman." In *Gender and Reading*. Ed. Elizabeth A. Flynn and Patrocinio P. Schweickart. Baltimore and London: Johns Hopkins University Press, 1986. Pp. 83-106.

Schweickart, Patrocinio P. "Reading Ourselves: Toward a Feminist Theory of Reading." In *Gender and Reading*. Ed. Elizabeth A. Flynn and Patrocinio P. Schweickart. Baltimore: Johns Hopkins University Press, 1986. Pp. 31-62.

Showalter, Elaine. "Feminist Criticism in the Wilderness." *Critical Inquiry*, 8 (1981), 182-5. Rpt. in *Writing and Sexual Difference*. Ed. Elizabeth Abel. Chicago: University of Chicago Press, 1980-2.

III. The Life and Works of Christine de Pizan
A. Primary Texts

The Book of the City of Ladies. Trans. Earl Jeffrey Richards. New York: Persea, 1982.

Selections from the the Debate over the *Romance of the Rose*. Trans. Charity Cannon Willard. In *Medieval Women Writers*. Ed. Katharina M. Wilson. Athens, Georgia: University of Georgia Press, 1984. Pp. 342-6.

_____ ("Christine's Response to the Treatise on the *Romance of the Rose* by John of Montreuil, June-July 1401: The First Extant Combative Document in the Debate"). Trans. Nadia Margolis. In *Medieval Women's Visionary Literature*. Ed. Elizabeth A. Petroff. New York: Oxford University Press, 1986. Pp. 340-6.

Landry, Geoffrey La Tour. *The Book of the Knight of the Tower*. Trans. William Caxton. Ed. M.Y. Offord. Early English Text Society, s.s. 2. London: Oxford University Press, 1971.

B. Secondary Texts

Bornstein, Diane, ed. *Ideals for Women in the Works of Christine de Pizan*. Detroit: Michigan Consortium for Medieval and Early Modern Studies, 1981.

Delaney, Sheila. "A city, a room: the scene of writing in Christine de Pisan and Virginia Woolf." In *Writing Women*: New York: Schocken, 1983. Pp. 181-97.

_____. "'Mothers to Think Back Through': Who are They? The Ambiguous Example of Christine de Pizan." In *Medieval Texts and Contemporary Readers*. Ed. Laurie A. Finke and Martin B. Schichtman. Ithaca: Cornell University Press, 1987. Pp. 177-97.

_____. "Rewriting Women Good: Gender and the Anxiety of Influence in Two Late-Medieval Texts." In *Chaucer in the Eighties*. Ed. Julian N. Wasserman and Robert J. Blanch. Syracuse: Syracuse University Press, 1986. Pp. 75-92.

Hindman, Sandra L. *Christine de Pizan's "Epistre Othea" : Painting and Politics at the Court of Charles VI.* Toronto: Pontifical Institute of Medieval Studies, 1986.

Huot, Sylvia. "Seduction and Sublimation: Christine de Pizan, Jean de Meun, and Dante." *Romance Notes,* 25 (1985), 361-73.

Ignatius, Mary Ann. "Christine de Pizan's *Epistre Othea*: An Experiment in Literary Form." *Medievalia et Humanistica,* 9 (1979), 127-42.

Kellogg, Judith. "Christine de Pisan as Chivalric Mythographer." In *The Mythographic Art: Classical Fable and the Rise of Vernacular Literature in Early France and England.* Ed. Jane Chance. Gainesville: University of Florida Press, forthcoming, 1990.

_____. *"Le Livre de la Cité des Dames*: Feminist Myth and Community," *Essays in Arts and Sciences,* forthcoming.

Kelly, Joan. "Early Feminist Theory and the *Querelle des Femmes.* 1400-1789." *Signs,* 8 (1982), 4-28.

Kennedy, Angus J. *Christine de Pizan: A Bibliographical Guide.* London: Grant and Cutler, Ltd., 1984.

McCleod, Enid. *The Order of the Rose, The Life and Ideas of Christine de Pizan.* Totowa, N. J.: Rowman and Littlefield, 1976.

Reno, Christine. "Feminist Aspects of Christine de Pizan's 'Epistre d'Othea a Hector.'" *Studi Francesi,* 71 (1980), 271- 76.

Schulenburg, Jane. "Clio's European Daughters: Myopic Modes of Perception." In *The Prism of Sex: Essays in the Sociology of Knowledge.* Ed. Julia Sherman and Evelyn Beck. Madison: University of Wisconsin Press, 1974. Pp. 33-53.

Tuve, Rosemond. *Allegorical Imagery.* Princeton: Princeton University Press, 1966. Pp. 33-45.

Willard, Charity C. *Christine de Pisan: Her Life and Works.* New York: Persea, 1984.

Yenal, Edith. *Christine de Pisan: A Bibliography of Writings by Her and About Her.* Metuchen, N. J.: Scarecrow, 1982.

Index of Proper Names

Numbers in parentheses refer to the numbers of the fables. *Pr.* stands for "Prologue." Anonymous authors are listed by title of work.

Lightning Source UK Ltd.
Milton Keynes UK
UKOW02f0839150317
296627UK00001B/13/P